basic

SPELLING

MICHAEL TEMPLE

JOHN MURRAY

Other titles in this series by Don Shiach:
Basic Grammar   ISBN 0 7195 7028 X
Basic Punctuation   ISBN 0 7195 7027 1
Basic Written English ISBN 0 7195 7030 1

Acknowledgements
The author and publishers wish to thank the following for permission to reproduce copyright material:

HarperCollins Publishers Ltd for extracts from Collins English Dictionary © William Collins Sons & Co Ltd 1979, 1985 and Collins Concise English Dictionary © William Collins Sons & Co Ltd 1982

Oxford University Press for extracts from the Oxford Study Dictionary (1991)

Heinemann Educational Books Ltd for an extract from the Heinemann English Dictionary © Heinemann Educational Books Ltd 1979

Longman Groups Ltd for an extract from the Longman's Concise Dictionary.

© Michael Temple 1995
First published 1995 by
John Murray (Publishers) Ltd
50 Albemarle Street
London W1X 4BD

Layouts by George Bowman
Illustrations by Art Construction and David Farris
Typeset by Servis Filmsetting Ltd, Manchester
Printed and bound in Great Britain by
The University Press, Cambridge

A CIP record for this book is available from the British Library.

ISBN 0 7195 7026 3

CONTENTS

CONTENTS

INTRODUCTION

WHY DOES SPELLING MATTER?

- Spelling is important for clear communication. It matters because it's such an obvious sign of competence in writing. It is one of the basic skills expected of all users of Standard English.
- Misspelling can be confusing, or at the very least, distracting for the reader. A badly spelt letter can put off a possible employer, and weak spelling can affect your performance in exams.
- Those who are unsure of their spelling often feel they have to choose simpler or more awkward expressions than they would like, or else they develop 'hang-ups' about writing generally.
- So what can be done? First of all, there is more logic to our spelling than you might think. There are rules or guidelines that account for the two 'm's or the two 't's in committee, for example. There are also several other rules that govern the spelling of many of our words.
- Once you begin to grasp the rules and start thinking about how words are formed, you'll soon have a 'word-building kit' that will enable you to cope with thousands of other 'difficult' words.
- This book offers a number of practical suggestions and well-tested methods, so that different spelling problems can be tackled separately by chapter and also in a structured way. To help you to remember words, rules and patterns, use the general strategies outlined in the following section. Then use the self-assessment questionnaire to check your own strengths and weaknesses in spelling before concentrating on the relevant chapters. Work your way through the Checkpoint exercises and Activities to practise each point. Answers to the Checkpoints and Activities are found at the end of the book.

GENERAL STRATEGIES: TEN KEYS TO BETTER SPELLING

1 Use this simple learning method: look, say, cover, write, check

- **Look** carefully at the word. Think about how it's made up. Underline the tricky bits.
- **Say** the word slowly, preferably aloud. Emphasise any slurred or unpronounced letters. Break longer words up into parts.
- **Cover** the word and try to picture the letters.
- **Write** the word slowly from memory.
- **Check** it against the original word letter by letter.

Take just a few words at a time. Start with the most common words and those you need most often. For instance, if you're writing a letter for a job, you'll need 'faithfully' or 'sincerely' and perhaps 'grateful' or 'interested'.

2 Break the word up and underline the key parts

- There is often a particular letter or part of the word that causes the problem. Write the word out and underline the problem part:

  recognise surprise separate undoubtedly

- Break longer words up into syllables or small bits, especially if sounds are slurred or unpronounced:

  Se-cret-ary, lab-or-at-ory, un-nec-ess-ary, part-ic-ul-arly

- Overstress the silent or slurred part:

  We**dnes**day vet**er-in-a**ry twel**f**th Feb**ru**ary

3 Use memory tips

For words you keep getting wrong, it's a good idea to use or invent a memory aid.

- A good **secret**ary keeps a **secret**.
- You **gain** with a bar**gain**.
- There's a **bus** in **bus**iness.
- There's a **para** (or **a rat**) in se**para**te.
- A p**ie**ce of p**ie**.
- Chew on this: there's **gum** in ar**gum**ent.
- The word fri**e**nd has the **e** near the **end**.

Try any memory aid that makes the spellings stick in your mind, no matter how odd it is. The main thing is for it to be easy to remember.

4 Keep a list

Keep a list of your own problem words in a little notebook. Ideally, use a book which has a section for each letter of the alphabet. Arranging words alphabetically makes them easy to check up on.

- It's best to include only common words **you** need most.
- Use it as a checklist and, in odd moments, learn a few at a time.
- Keys 5, 6 and 7 below will together make up a Word-building Kit.

5 Use a dictionary (See Chapter 4.)
Ask anyone you like if he or she can spell desiccated or, even more difficult, syzygy (pronounced sisserjee)! The point is that **everyone** needs to use a dictionary, and not only to check spelling. Choose one carefully, comparing different editions. Spend a little time studying the introduction: this will explain the layout, symbols and abbreviations, so you'll be able to make full use of the dictionary. If possible, buy a fairly large dictionary that gives the origins of words. Remember that a good dictionary is an investment for life.

6 Take notice of word-families and roots (See Chapter 5.)
A good dictionary will provide you with other words in the same family. For example, the word medicine is related to the word medical and this fact should help you remember the 'i' after the 'd'.

Knowing the origin or root of a word can make sense of the spelling. The word biscuit, for instance, contains the French word for cooked (cuit) and the word 'bis' which means twice.

Once you get to know the main prefixes and suffixes too, you'll be able to connect the spelling of a word with its meaning. (See Chapters 5–7.) An ante-room (ante – meaning before) is a room that comes before or leads into a larger room. Antiseptic (anti – meaning against) acts against infection.

7 Learn the rules for word formation (See Chapters 5–10.)
These are covered in the main chapters of this book. The self-assessment questionnaire on pages 6–9 has been arranged so that you can isolate or focus on those rules or guidelines that you personally need to work at. Take these slowly, bit by bit, and refer to them when in doubt.

Remember that grasping these rules will go a long way to solving most of your spelling problems.

8 Drafting, proofreading and clear handwriting
- When writing anything important, such as a letter applying for a job, it's best to do a plan and write a rough draft.
- Write neatly and clearly as this, in itself, will help you spell more carefully. (Sometimes people hide their uncertain spelling under illegible or untidy handwriting!)
- **Check** any word you're unsure of in a dictionary. Give special attention to accident black spots like its/it's or affect/effect or past/passed. (If you use a word-processor don't rely entirely on a spell-check.)
- Remember, too, that if you write a word down wrongly a few times it can start to 'look right' (and be harder to correct later).

9 Keep your eyes open
- **Look** carefully at words around you, wherever they are – on cornflake packets, in advertisements, on the television screen. Try to get used to the 'look' of the word.
- **Think** about the **meaning** of the word (especially when there's danger of confusion as with who's/whose or principal/principle).

10 Learn the 250 key words (See Chapter 13.)
These are the most commonly misspelt words. Know them and you'll solve a high percentage of your spelling problems.

Refer to the lists often and gradually work at all the key words, using the learning methods in keys 1 and 2 above.

Note: The activities at the end of each chapter and in *Further activities* (Chapter 14) have been designed for use in class or for private study. Many of them could be used as dictations. Answers to all the activities and to the Self-assessment questionnaire on page 6 are at the end of the book.

TERMS YOU NEED TO KNOW

VOWELS   The letters a, e, i, o, u are called vowels. (The letter 'y' is a vowel when it sounds like 'i', as in try or gypsy.)

CONSONANTS   All letters except a, e, i, o, u are consonants. (The letter 'y' is a consonant in words like yes and beyond.)

SYLLABLE   A syllable is a single sound made with one push of the breath. The word mischievous (mis–chiev–ous) has three syllables, while the word inspect (in–spect) has two.

STRESS   The stress is the emphasis put on a certain part of a word when you say it. In the word ad**mit** the stress is on the 'mit', while **or**bit has the stress on the 'or'.

BASE WORD   This is a complete word to which you can add parts to make other words, for example, the word **pay** is the base word in re**pay**ment.

ROOT   This is the stem or basic part of a word, for example, **rupt** is the root in **rupt**ure and inter**rupt**.

PREFIX   This is a group of letters (or a letter) added to the **front** of a word or root to change its meaning, for example, the prefix **pre** (meaning 'in front' or 'before') in the words **pre**fix and **pre**pare.

SUFFIX   This is a group of letters (or a letter) added to the **end** of a word or root to change its meaning or use. Two examples are the suffix **-ness** added to stubborn to make stubborn**ness** and the suffix **-ment** added to achieve to make achieve**ment**.

VOWEL-SUFFIXES and CONSONANT-SUFFIXES   Suffixes like **-ing**, **-able** and **-ed** that **begin** with a **vowel** are called **vowel**-suffixes. Suffixes like **-ness** and **-ment** that **begin** with a **consonant** are called **consonant**-suffixes.

SINGULAR   This is the form of the word used when there is only one:
a book   a child

PLURAL   This is the form of the word used when there is more than one:
books   children

▌ THE MAIN PARTS OF SPEECH

- A NOUN is a word that names a thing, a person, a place, or an idea or feeling:
  brick   boy   mountain   beauty   guilt
  A PROPER NOUN names a **particular** thing, person, place or time. It has a capital letter:
  John   Spain   Tuesday

- A PRONOUN stands in place of a noun to avoid repeating it:
  he   him   she   it   they   who

- A VERB is a word that expresses an action (or state of being):
  He **ran**.   She **is** friendly.
  A verb has several 'tenses' showing present, past or future time.

- An ADJECTIVE is a word that describes or gives more information about a noun or pronoun:
  She is a **clever** politician.   He was **angry**.

- An ADVERB is a word that gives more information about a verb, or an adjective, or another adverb:
  He ran **quickly**   **very** good   **extremely** badly

5

SELF-ASSESSMENT QUESTIONNAIRE

This questionnaire is designed to help you identify your strengths and weaknesses in spelling, so that you can then concentrate on the chapters in the book that are the most appropriate for you.

Each quiz contains 30 spellings. Answers are on page 111. (Alternatively, the words in the quizzes can be dictated to you.)

1 Choose the right word to put in the gaps.
  a We don't (no/know) .... (were/where/we're) .... (were/where/we're) .... going.
  b Are (there/their/they're) .... friends (there/their/they're) ...., (to/too/two) ....?
  c (Theirs/there's) .... no doubt that it is (past/passed) .... her bedtime.
  d I wonder (who's/whose) .... car that is and (who's/whose) .... parked it like that.
  e Is this (your/you're) .... doing? Look what (your/you're) .... doing!
  f It is far (to/too/two) .... hot (to/too/two) .... go (to/too/two) .... the cinema.
  g A piece (of/off/have) .... slate must (of/off/have) .... fallen (of/off/have) .... the roof.
  h The injury didn't seem to have any (affect/effect) .... on her performance since she was still first (past/passed) .... the winning post.
  i (Let's/Lets) .... consider the (principal/principle) .... reasons for going.
  j They will all (accept/except) .... the invitation (accept/except) .... John.
  k The cat was (quiet/quite) .... (quiet/quite) .... hoping to (loose/lose) .... the dog by (laying/lying) .... low under the bushes.
  l I (hear/here) .... that you were (allowed/aloud) .... to go to the party.
(See Chapter 1.)

2 a Making any necessary spelling changes to these words,
  (i) add **-ing** to dine .... shine .... stun .... panic .... pursue ....
  (ii) add **-ous** to courage .... advantage ....
  (iii) add **-able** to notice .... manage ....

6

(iv) add **-ed** to picnic .... wrap .... pin ....
plan .... mimic ....

b Insert **ie** or **ei** in these:

rec _ _ ve retr _ _ ve fr _ _ ndly n _ _ ghbours c _ _ ling ach _ _ ve
s _ _ ze w _ _ ght h _ _ ght conc _ _ ted n _ _ ce ch _ _ f
bel _ _ ve h _ _ rloom rel _ _ ve perc _ _ ve

(See Chapter 2.)

3 How many of these are correct? Rewrite them correctly where necessary.

a biznez	intresting	envolved ....
b medcine	mischeivious	burglar ....
c vegtable	litrature	discription ....
d twelth	century	contempary ....
e genrally	secketery	reckernise ....
f luxery	temprature	primmative ....
g fastening	desparate	enviroment ....
h athletics	particulerly	peculierley ....
i nessecary	Febuary	interlectual ....
j dissintegrate	library	undoubtly ....

(See Chapter 3.)

4 Fill in the missing letters.

a di ...... ppoint   di ...... appear   di ...... imilar (not 'similar)

b wit ...... old (hold back)   inte ...... uption   a ...... nowledge (admit)

c proc ...... d (go along)   i ...... ediate (now)   o ...... onent (enemy)

d co ...... otion (noise)   fo ...... court (area in front of a garage)
a ...... uire (obtain)

e ove ...... ule   a ...... ression (force)   con ...... ous (aware, awake)

f defin ...... te   i ...... egible (unreadable)   ac ...... modation

g en ...... mous (huge)   r ...... diculous   su ...... ose (reckon)

h we ...... fare   ant ...... dote   ski ...... ful

i u ...... atural (not natural)   sep ...... rate   s ...... prise (shock)

j de ...... nd (go down)   a ...... laim (declare)   i ...... odest (lacking modesty)

(See Chapter 5.)

5 a Fill in the blanks with one or two letters.

(i) drunke _ _ ess   notic _ _ ng   stubbor _ _ ess

(ii) manag _ _ ble   achiev _ _ ent   marr _ _ age (being married)

(iii) vig _ _ rous   arg _ _ ing   purs _ _ ing

(iv) car _ _ ng (taking care)   gover _ _ ent
admir _ _ ng

(v) excit _ _ ent   hum _ _ rous   slop _ _ ng (from slope)

b Put **i** or **y** in these blanks.

(i) hungr _ ly	lonel _ ness	surve _ ing
(ii) tid _ ness	likel _ hood	suppl _ ing
(iii) cop _ ed	wear _ ness	bus _ ness
(iv) livel _ ness	l _ ing (resting)	happ _ ness
(v) gidd _ ness	shabb _ ness	mood _ ness

(See Chapter 6.)

6 Add **-ing** to all of these, making any necessary spelling changes:

a swim	begin	transfer ....
b submit	scare	omit ....
c rivet	orbit	profit ....
d develop	murmur	appal ....
e benefit	happen	quarrel ....
f commit	propel	gallop ....
g offer	travel	pocket ....
h occur	worship	conceal ....
i regret	prefer	forget ....
j refer	permit	ballot ....

(See Chapter 7.)

7 Make adverbs (words ending in **-ly**) from these. Make any necessary spelling changes; for example, the word lazy would become lazily.

a exception	fantastic	extraordinary ....
b cool	drastic	public ....
c incidental	immediate	accidental ....
d true	sincere	simple ....
e dramatic	probable	faithful ....
f automatic	happy	whole ....
g tragic	terrific	humble ....
h careful	subtle	real ....
i unnecessary	peculiar	similar ....
j frantic	extreme	normal ....

(See Chapter 8.)

8 a Fill in the gaps in these words:

cemet _ ry imagin _ ry cent _ ry relev _ nt independ _ nt
eleg _ nt magnific _ nt excell _ nt visit _ r famili _ r govern _ r
solicit _ r peculi _ r gramm _ r calend _ r

b Make words ending in **-ible** or **-able** from these; for example, return would become returnable:

response	agree	value ....
notice	change	collapse ....

c Make words ending in **-ous** from these:

marvel	religion	luxury ....
mischief	outrage	humour ....
disaster	advantage	glamour ....

(See Chapter 9.)

9 Write out the plural of these; for example, book (one, singular) would become books (plural, more than one):

a lady .... thief .... tomato ....
b bench .... valley .... chief ....
c glass .... supply .... wife ....
d chimney .... shelf .... survey ....
e ally .... volley .... business ....
f lay-by .... hero .... pony ....
g potato .... library .... phenomenon ....
h child .... send-off .... crisis ....
i spoonful .... lorry .... roof ....
j factory .... gas .... witness ....

(See Chapters 10 and 11.)

10 a Which is correct?
tomorrow/to morrow   upstairs/up stairs   straightaway/straight away   where as/whereas   aswell/as well   in fact/infact   inspite of/in spite of   shortterm/short-term   american/American   doesn't/doesnt   childrens toys/children's toys

b Write these sentences out correctly:
(i) Our local stationers seems to sell alot of christmas gift's and childrens games, where as your's dosent.
(ii) Inspiteof all the english teams efforts to re-cover there lost form, noone managed to score, all though the team was playing infront of a home crowd.
(iii) The Womens Institute has, infact, all ready held it's annual meeting.

(See Chapter 12.)

Check your answers against those given on page 111. Add up your total score for each execise.
Score 28 out of 30: well done – but if you didn't get them all right you should brush up on one or two points in the chapter concerned.
Score between 25 and 27: good going, but you should check up on a few spelling tips and rules in the relevant chapters.
Score between 20 and 24: not bad, but you will certainly benefit from a study of the chapters concerned.
Score below 20: you can only improve by studying the appropriate chapters. Work through them carefully.

1

WORDS OFTEN CONFUSED

- It will be helpful, when working through this chapter, to remember that a noun is a word that names a thing, person, place or quality, whilst a verb is a word that expresses an action.
- Do you ever mix up its and it's or who's and whose? And how about principal and principle and affect and effect?
- Words like these are confused because they sound or look alike. Even if you know the difference it's easy to make the kind of mistake we call 'a slip of the pen'.
- The best approach is to think firstly about the **meaning** of the word you want. Secondly, give these words special attention when checking through what you have written.

LIST OF COMMONLY CONFUSED WORDS

Here is a checklist, in alphabetical order, of the most commonly confused words. Special exercises are included at the end of the chapter for the words set in capital letters.

ACCEPT (to receive)   *I accept your kind offer.*

EXCEPT (not including, also to exclude)   *All except one were saved.*

advice (noun, rhymes with nice)   *a piece of good advice*

advise (verb, rhymes with wise)   *I advise you to use a dictionary.*

AFFECT (verb, meaning to alter, cause a change)   *Smoking can affect your health.*

EFFECT (noun, meaning a result; also verb meaning to bring about)   *The effect of the medicine was amazing.*   *He effected his escape with ease.*

ALLOWED (permitted)   *No dogs allowed on the beach.*

ALOUD (out loud)   *You're thinking aloud.*

almost (nearly)   *We almost won.*

all most   *They were all most helpful (meaning, everyone was).*

already (by now)   *I already know this.*

all ready   *Are you all ready? (meaning, is everyone?)*

alright (OK)   *Are those peaches alright?*

all right   *The answers are all right (meaning, each one is correct).*

altogether (completely)   *I do not altogether approve.*

all together (all are together)   *I have put these papers all together.*

always (every time)   *I always check carefully.*

all ways (all methods or routes)   *All ways are closed.*

anyway (in any case)   *I intend to visit him anyway.*

any way (any single way or means)   *I can't think of any way to do it.*

bare (adjective meaning naked; also verb meaning to uncover)   *a bare chest; to bare all*

bear (an animal; also verb meaning to suffer)   *teddy bear; I grin and bear it.*

beach   *sandy beach*

beech   *beech tree*

boarder (lodger)   *a weekly boarder at a boarding-school*

border (edge, frontier)   *the border between France and Spain*

brake (noun and verb)   *Slam on your brakes. He always brakes hard.*

break (noun and verb)   *tea break; she breaks the mirror.*

breath (noun)   *Take a deep breath.*

breathe (verb)   *Breathe through your nose.*

canvas (a fabric)   *The canvas on the tent was torn.*

canvass (to ask for votes)   *The candidate canvassed for votes.*

cereal (grain, cornflakes)   *My children will only eat one kind of cereal.*

serial (part of a series or set)   *the longest running serial on TV*

check (noun or adjective meaning a pattern of squares; verb meaning to test or to stop)   *a checked skirt; check your spelling.*

cheque (bank draft or bill)   *Pay by cheque.*

choose (rhymes with snooze)   *I choose to live alone.*

chose (past tense – rhymes with nose)   *I chose one yesterday.*

clothes (garments)   *Wear casual clothes.*

cloths (rhymes with moths)   *washing-up cloths*

coarse (rough, crude)   *coarse fishing, coarse behaviour, coarse cloth*

course (golf course; part of a meal; series; of course)   *a course in yoga*

complement (verb meaning to complete; noun meaning that which makes up)   *ship's complement or crew*

compliment (noun and verb meaning praise)   *pay a compliment*

council/councillor (assembly, member of assembly)   *Town Council*

counsel/counsellor (noun meaning advice; verb meaning to advise; adviser)   *Counsel for the Defence*

currant (berry) *blackcurrant*

current (adjective meaning now running; noun meaning stream or flow) *current affairs; river current; electric current*

dairy (where milk is produced) *cows in a dairy*

diary (daily account) *The Diary of Anne Frank*

desert (noun meaning barren place, what you deserve; verb meaning to abandon) *Sahara Desert, your just deserts; desert your country*

dessert *chocolate dessert*

draft (rough plan) *bank draft, overdraft*

draught *draught of air, beer on draught; ship's draught; game of draughts*

drawer *chest of drawers*

draw (noun meaning tied game, attraction; verb meaning to pull, to draw with a pencil) *He had eight draws on his football pools coupon.*

dual (two) *dual controls, dual carriageway*

duel *a fencing duel*

emigrant (one who leaves a country to live elsewhere)

immigrant (one who comes to live in a country)

eminent (distinguished, important) *an eminent person*

imminent (threatening, about to happen) *imminent disaster, imminent arrival*

enquiry/enquire (noun meaning a request for information; verb meaning to ask for information) *Enquire about the forms at your local Post Office.*

inquiry/inquire (noun meaning an official investigation; also verb meaning to carry out such an investigation) *An inquiry was set up into the murder.*

ensure (to make sure) *Please ensure that you enclose a cheque.*

insure (to take out an insurance policy) *The driver was not insured.*

flowed (of water) *Water flowed swiftly*

flown (of birds, aircraft) *The birds have flown.*

formally *Dress formally for a formal occasion.*

formerly (before, previously referred to) *he was formerly prime minister; formerly and latterly*

HEAR (with your EAR) *to hear him coming*

HERE (over here not over there – compare here, there, where)   *Come here.*

heroin (drug)   *to take heroin*

heroine (brave woman or main character)   *She behaved like a heroine.*

hoard (of treasure)   *a hoard of silver coins; she hoarded food.*

horde (a pack)   *hordes of shoppers*

IT'S (short for it is or it has); compare with I'm, he's (he is), she's (she is)   *It's late. It's mine. It's gone.*

ITS (belonging to it; compare with my, your, his, her)   *the country and its people*

LAY (to put something down flat)   *Lay the table. Lay an egg.* (The past tense is LAID.)

LIE (to rest)   *I am going to lie down.* (The past tenses are LAY and have LAIN.)

lead (rhymes with feed, verb meaning to take along, or noun; or, when it rhymes with head, means the metal)   *Lead the way; dog on a lead; as heavy as lead*

led (rhymes with bed; the past tense of to lead)   *He led them all a merry dance.*

leant (past tense of to lean)   *She leant out of the window.*

lent (past tense of to lend)   *He lent me a fiver.*

LET'S (short for let us)   *Let's all go down the Strand.*

LETS (the verb form used with he, she or it)   *He lets us do as we please.*

licence (noun)   *a driving or dog licence*

license (verb)   *to license a vehicle*

lightening (making lighter)   *lightening a load*

lightning   *a flash of lightning*

LOOSE (rhymes with goose)   *His shoe-lace, or tooth, was loose.*

LOSE (rhymes with shoes)   *to lose your pen or lose the game*

manner (way)   *in a manner of speaking*

manor (house)   *a manor house*

maybe (perhaps)   *Maybe I'll come.*

may be   *They may be arriving tomorrow.*

meter   *gas or parking meter*

metre   *a 100-metre race*

new   *new for old; the news*

knew   *She knew my brother.*

no   *yes and no*

know   *Didn't you know the answer?*

OF (pronounced 'ov', meaning belonging to, relating to or by)   *The Wizard of Oz, a question of money, a favourite of mine; of course*

OFF (rhymes with cough, meaning away from or down from a place)   *He fell off the cliff.*

HAVE   *I must have made a mistake. (This can be shortened to I must've ...
but **never** use 'of' as a verb.)*

PASSED (the past tense of the verb to pass)   *He has passed his exams. She
passed me the butter. Time passed slowly.*

PAST (for all other uses and meanings)   *in the past; past civilisations; the
lorries hurtled past; he ran past me.*

peace   *war and peace*

piece (a bit)   *a piece of pie*

personal (private)   *a personal matter*

personnel (employees or staff)   *the personnel manager*

plain (flat country; clear, undecorated, unattractive)   *Salisbury Plain; make it
plain*

plane (verb meaning to make level; also noun meaning a tool, a tree)   *He
planed the wood smooth. She sat under a plane tree.*

PRACTICE (noun)   *games practice*

PRACTISE (verb)   *You need to practise your spelling.*

pray (worship, ask for – as in 'prayer')   *Let us pray for a miracle.*

prey (noun meaning a hunted animal; verb meaning to hunt down)   *The cat
chased its prey. The lion preys on the antelope.*

PRINCIPAL (chief)   *the college principal; the principal features of towns*

PRINCIPLE (rule, law, moral values)   *the principle of the thing*

prophecy (noun; pronounced 'see' at the end)   *a prophecy of doom*

prophesy (verb; pronounced 'eye' at the end)   *to prophesy*

QUIET   *Be quiet! peace and quiet*

QUITE (rhymes with bite)   *quite a handful; quite right*

seam (joined edges or line)   *sew a seam on a dress; coal seam*

seem (to appear)   *These all seem to be OK.*

sew (past tense: sewn)   *sew stitches, clothes*

sow (past tense: sown)   *sow lettuce seeds*

sure (certain)   *Are you absolutely sure?*

shore   *the sea shore*

sometimes (now and then)   *I sometimes go to the cinema.*

some times (some particular times)   *There are some times when nothing
goes right.*

shear (to cut)   *to shear a sheep*

sheer (utter; perpendicular)   *sheer madness; a sheer drop; sheer stockings*

sight (sometimes seen)   *a sight for sore eyes*

site (place)   *camp site, building site*

THEIR (belonging to them)   *They have their own opinions.*

THERE (not here; there is, there are, etc.)   *Look over there.*

THEY'RE (they are)   *They're off!*

THEIRS (something belonging to them)   *Theirs is the red car.*

1

THERE'S (there is or there has)   *There's no chance of rain. There's been none for ages.*

tire (to weary, also to wear out)   *The child will tire soon. The conversation will tire the old lady.*

tyre   *a punctured tyre*

TO   (towards; in order to; and in the verb-form to sing, to play etc.)

TOO (excessively; as well)   *too hot; You come, too.*

TWO (the number 2)

threw   *He threw the discus.*

through (by means of; in one end and out the other)

waist   *a 24 inch waist*

waste   *waste disposal*

weather (rain, sun, fog, etc.)   *What lovely weather!*

whether (if)   *I wonder whether he'll come.*

WE'RE (rhymes with beer; meaning we are)   *We're playing Leeds tomorrow.*

WERE (rhymes with fur; the past tense of are)   *We were in Scotland last year.*

WHERE (rhymes with air, meaning in what place)   *Where are you going? I know where it is.*

WHO'S (who is; who has)   *Who's that? Who's borrowed my pen?*

WHOSE (belonging to whom)   *Whose case is that? I know whose it is.*

wander (to roam about)

wonder (to guess)

YOU'RE (you are)   *You're looking well.*

YOUR (belonging to you)   *It's your choice.*

(See also Chapter 12 for words like re-cover/recover, re-sign/resign, re-form/reform.)

✓ *Checkpoint*

Revise carefully all the words in capital letters in the list above.

1 Choose the right word for each space.
  a (Whose/Who's) .... is it? (Its/It's) .... mine.
  b (Lets/Let's) .... see. (There/Their/They're) .... you are then.
  c But (your/you're) .... cheating. (Theirs/There's) .... nothing (their/there/they're)............ . (We're/Were/Where) .... did you hide it?
  d I don't (know/no) .... It must (have/of/off) .... slipped (threw/through) .... my fingers.

2 Put **their**, **there** or **they're** in the spaces:
.... is no doubt that .... singing is not what .... famous for.

15

3 Put **past** or **passed** in the spaces:
He had already gone .... me before he .... me the ball.

4 Put **lose** or **loose** in the spaces:
This tooth is so .... that I shall probably .... it.

5 Put **lets** or **let's** in the spaces:
If he .... us then .... do it.

6 Put **to**, **too** or **two** in the spaces:
There were .... many for all of us .... have a game.

7 Put **accept** or **except** in the spaces:
They agreed to .... all the entries .... mine.

8 Put **practice** or **practise** in the spaces:
.... makes perfect, so make sure you ....

9 Put **lying**, **laying**, **laid** or **lain** in the spaces:
Yesterday he was .... in the bed where he had .... for the past two weeks, but today the nurses have .... him on a sunbed outside.

10 Put **principal** or **principle** in the spaces:
His .... concern was for the moral .... involved in the case.

Activities 1–6

1 Choose the right word to insert in the gaps.
  a Drivers should carry a (current/currant) .... driving (license/licence) .... , (cheque/check) .... (tires/tyres) .... and (breaks/brakes) .... frequently, and (ensure/insure) .... that the boot and all doors are locked when the car is (stationery/stationary) .... Remember that wet conditions will (affect/effect) .... (breaking/braking) .... and remember to use the mirror especially on (duel/dual) .... carriageways and motorways. Don't forget that tiredness and stress are among the (principle/principal) .... causes of road accidents.
  b Having (past/passed) .... all her drama exams, Tracey (lead/led) .... a relatively (quiet or quite) .... life for a while before being given the (role/roll) .... of (principal/principle) .... boy in pantomine. Further parts followed in comic (reviews/revues) .... until she landed a (plum/plumb) .... part in a popular television (cereal/serial) ....

2 Choose the right word from the pair to fill in the gaps in each advertisement.
  a stationery/stationary
    The perfect Christmas gift – personalised ....
    Is your business .... ? We'll get you on the move!
  b cereal/serial
    The only .... with 60 per cent fruit!
    Don't miss Channel 4's exciting new ....
  c review/revue
    Is it time to .... your finances? Talk to us!
    For a hilarious night out – nothing better than an evening of
    comic ....
  d role/roll
    A brilliant piece of theatre with stars in all the major .... s.
    It's no party without Mini-Savoury .... s!

3 Choose the right word from the pair to complete these newspaper headlines:
  a moral/morale

> **Is this the party of high .... standards?**

> **............ among back-benchers at an all-time low**

  b Britain/Briton

> **............ and Europe – how many miles apart?**

> **Six .... s killed in air crash over Japan**

  c idol/idle

> **Teenage .... dies of overdose**

> **Minister calls homeless '............'.**

4 Write a letter that includes all of the following words:
  here   hear   its   it's   effect   affect   let's   you're

5 Think about the pronunciation and spelling of the following pairs of words
  and explain the difference in meaning:
  dose/doze   disease/decease   envelop/envelope   differ/defer

6 Write a short description of an event (about half a page) using the following
  words, in any order:
  its   affect   lose   passed

2

PRONUNCIATION AS A HELP TO SPELLING

- **Say these words aloud:**
  hop hope pan pane shin shine slop slope
- **Vowels (a, e, i, o, u and sometimes 'y') can be pronounced 'long', as in hope and pane or 'short' (as in hop or pan).**
- **The vowel sounds in cap, pet, sit, hop, cut and holly are short.**
- **The vowel sounds in cape, Pete, site, hope, cute and try are long.**
- **The spelling in these cases is a guide to correct pronunciation.**

LONG AND SHORT VOWELS

The silent 'e' at the ends of words like hope and tape means that we pronounce the previous vowel sound **long**. (In hop and tap the vowel sounds are 'short'.)

long: stripe pine robe
short: strip pin rob

Now what happens when we add **vowel**-suffixes (like -ing and -ed) to these two sets of words?

RULE When **vowel**-suffixes (like -ing and -ed) are added to words ending in a **silent 'e'**, the **silent 'e'** is dropped:
hope → hoping tape → taping

Further examples:
- adding -ing: glide → gliding shine → shining come → coming dine → dining
- adding -ed: glide →glided grate → grated skate → skated

This also applies to words of more than one syllable like describe and amaze:

describe → describing　decide → deciding　amaze → amazing
approve → approving

Note that this rule does **not** apply when **consonant**-suffixes (like -less, -ful, -ment) are added:

hope+less → hopeless　hope+ful → hopeful
engage+ment → engagement

(See also the next section below.)

Occasionally the silent 'e' will stay:

- rateable, saleable – here the 'e' emphasises the long 'a' in the base words 'rate', 'sale'
- dyeing (colouring), singeing (burning), re-routeing – this avoids confusion with dying (dead), singing, routing (defeating)
- in words ending in 'oe' like canoeing, hoeing, toeing

✓ *Checkpoint A*

1 Add **-ing** to these:
  a mate ....
  b snipe ....
  c decline ....
  d shake ....
  e admire ....
  f amuse ....
  g write ....
  h interfere ....
  i argue ....

2 Add **-ed** to these:
  a care ....
  b arrive ....
  c stripe ....
  d queue ....

3 Add **-ful** to these:
  a care ....
  b fate ....
  c disgrace ....
  d shame ....

■ ADDING VOWEL-SUFFIXES TO ONE-SYLLABLE WORDS ENDING IN ONE SHORT VOWEL AND A CONSONANT

What happens when we add **-ing** or **-ed** to words like tap, hop, pin, stun and slim, all words that contain just one 'short' vowel sound?

> **RULE** When **vowel**-suffixes are added to one-syllable words ending in a vowel and a single consonant, the final consonant must be **doubled**:
>
> tap → tapped, tapping
> hop → hopped, hopping

BUT I THOUGHT YOU SAID YOU WERE *STRIPPED* TO THE WAIST!

Further examples: pin → pinning stun → stunning slim → slimming
skip → skipped

This rule does **not** apply when **consonant**-suffixes are added:
cup → cupful sad → sadness wit → witless

✓ *Checkpoint B*

1 Add **-ing** to these:
  a snip ....
  b skin ....
  c rob ....
  d sit ....

2 Add **-ed** to these:
  a pat ....
  b rot ....
  c bat ....
  d skim ....

Contrast:
• after a long vowel, drop the silent 'e' – I'd love to recline in a reclining chair
• after a short vowel, double the final consonant – He took a pin and pinned the photo to the wall.

Exceptions:
- words ending in w, x and y – renewing   fixed   delayed
- words ending in more than one vowel and a consonant – awaiting appeared
- words ending in two consonants – rewarding   sanded   builder

---

✓ *Checkpoint C*

---

1 Add **-er** and **-ing** to these:
  a wrap ....
  b recline ....
  c rob ....
  d debate ....

2 Add **-ing** to these:
  a win ....
  b whine ....
  c wipe ....
  d whip ....
  e pursue ....
  f hit ....

ADDING VOWEL-SUFFIXES TO LONGER WORDS

Look at these words:
   begin   target   refer   offer
All of them end in a single vowel and a single consonant.

Now pronounce the same words. Where is the stress? On the first or the last syllable? If you are unsure, try over-emphasising the vowel. For example, in be**gin** the stress is on the last syllable.

Now look at and pronounce these words:
   beginning   targeting   referring   offering
These words are examples of the following rule.

> **RULE** For words of more than one syllable ending in just one vowel and one consonant:
>
> when adding **vowel**-suffixes (like -ing, -ed), the last letter is **doubled only** if the stress is at the **end**.

Where is the stress in these words?
   happen   occur   gallop   admit   offer   refer
- If the stress is at the **end**, double: occ**ur**ring   adm**it**ted   ref**er**ring
- If the stress is **not** at the end, don't double: h**a**ppening   g**a**lloped **o**ffering

Exceptions:

- words ending in 'w', 'x', and 'y' – renewing   relaxed   delayed
- words ending in more than one vowel and a consonant – awaiting appeared
- words ending in two consonants – rewarding   sanded

Where is the stress in these words? Note how the different spellings depend on the stress.

prefer preferred preference
refer referring reference

- The above rule does not apply when **consonant**-suffixes are added, like -ment, -ness, for example, preferment.

Note that focus and bias may be spelled with or without doubling the 's' when a vowel-suffix is added.

✓ *Checkpoint D*

Choose the right word below and give it the correct ending. (If in doubt, pronounce the base word and think about which rule applies.)

1 Add **-ed** to these:

  a He (bare/bar) .... his chest to the elements.
     The way was (bare/bar) ....

  b The road (slope/slop) .... gently down the hill.
     He (slope/slop) .... water all over the table.

  c She (plane/plan) .... her essay carefully.
     The carpenter (plane/plan) .... the piece of wood.

  d His hair was all (mat/mate) ....
     The two pandas eventually (mat/mate) ....

  e She was (scare/scar) .... of spiders.
     The cut on the face (scare/scar) .... him for life.

  f She (strip/stripe) .... the pine table of its old varnish.
     He preferred the (strip/stripe) ....jumper.

  g She (pin/pine) .... away with grief.
     He (pin/pine) .... the card on the board.

2 Add **-ing** to these:

  a The boxers were (spare/spar) .... in the ring.
     They were (spare/spar) .... no expense.

  b They all enjoyed the (wine/win) .... and (dine/din) ....
     By (dine/din) .... tactics into the team the coach helped them to start (wine/win) ....

  c The bosun was (pipe/pip) .... the captain aboard.
     He won the race by just (pipe/pip) .... his rival at the post.

✓ Checkpoint E

1 Add **-ing** to these:
   a fasten ....
   b profit ....
   c occur ....
   d fidget ....
   e confer ....

2 Add **-ed** to these:
   a permit ....
   b prohibit ....
   c deter ....
   d regret ....
   e target ....
   f benefit ....

■ WORDS ENDING IN ONE VOWEL + 'l'

> **RULE** When words end in one vowel + **'l'**, the 'l' is doubled when **vowel**-suffixes are added. It doesn't matter where the stress is in this case:
>
> cancel → cancelled, cancellation   travel → traveller, travelling
> propel → propelled   equal → equalled   fulfil → fulfilling

Exceptions: when adding -ise or -ize (or -iser/-izer) and -ity, for example, civilise   tranquiliser   civility   equality (but not tranquillity)

Further exceptions: (un)paralleled parallelogram

Note that this rule does not apply when adding **consonant**-suffixes

- to words like enrol → enrolment
- to words ending in a double vowel plus consonant like appeal → appealing   reveal → revealing

✓ Checkpoint F

1 Add -ing and -ise to equal   ....
2 Add -some and -ing to quarrel   ....
3 Add -ise and -ity to real   ....
4 Add -ed and -ing to label   ....
5 Add -ed and -ous to marvel   ....
6 Add -ing and -ity to total   ....
7 Add -ent and -ed to excel   ....

IS IT 'IE' OR 'EI'?

There is a well-known rhyme that helps you with 'ie' and 'ei', but you need to remember that it applies when the sound is 'ee'.

> **RULE** I before E
> except after C
> **if the sound is EE**: chief   receive

Read these headlines, paying special attention to the words containing the 'ee' sound, and see how they follow the above rule.

> *Besieged victims receive brief message from friends*

> *Niece's piece of deceit is hard to believe*

> **Best achievement in the field**

> **Finance chief hits the ceiling**

The other side of this rule is just as useful:

> **RULE** If the sound is not 'ee', the spelling is 'ei'.

Here are some more newspaper headline examples:

> **Neighbours welcome foreign heiress**

> **Styles for any weight or height!**

WE'RE WEIRD!

Exception: (not pronounced 'ee') – friend.
Remember: 'Fri**end**s to the **end**'.

Other main exceptions: SEIZE   weir(d)

Other exceptions: protein   counterfeit
plebeian   caffeine   species

✓ *Checkpoint G*

Use the above rule to insert **ie** or **ei** in these:
1 rel _ _ f
2 sover _ _ gn
3 l _ _ sure
4 conc _ _ ted
5 sh _ _ ld

6 w _ _ ght
7 handkerch _ _ f
8 fr _ _ ght
9 gr _ _ f

THE SOFT AND HARD 'C' AND 'G'

Pronounce these words: civil   cattle   general   gallop   ceiling   giraffe
goat   cot

The 'c' and 'g' are pronounced 'soft' (like 's' and 'j' sounds) in civil, ceiling, general and giraffe but are pronounced 'hard' (like 'k' and the 'g' in goat) in cattle and gallop.

The tendency is for the 'c' and 'g' to be soft when followed by 'e' or 'i' and 'hard' when followed by 'a', 'o' and 'u'.

> **RULE** When adding suffixes like -able and -ous to words ending in -ce and -ge (like notice and courage), we need to keep the silent 'e' so that the sound stays **soft**: notice → noticeable
> courage → courageous   knowledge → knowledgeable
> manage → manageable   advantage → advantageous

Note that the letter 'i' after a 'c' or 'g' has a softening effect. For instance, the 'i' in religious and vicious keeps the 'g' and 'c' soft.

The normal rule with long-vowelled words is to drop the silent 'e' when adding -ing or -ed:

   price → pricing   rage → raging

(See *Long and short vowels*, page 18.)

Exceptions: whingeing   singeing (burning)   ageing

> **RULE** If we want the 'c' to stay 'hard' (like a 'k') when adding suffixes beginning with 'i' or 'e' (like -ing or -ed), we need to insert a 'k'.

PICNICKING PANIC!
Four picnickers were panicked into abandoning their picnic yesterday when a raging bull charged towards them. . .

Further examples: traffic → trafficking   mimic → mimicking
bivouac → bivouacked   tarmac → tarmacked

Note that a 'u' after a 'g' often indicates a 'hard' sound:
guest   guide   guardian   fatigue   intrigue   vogue

✓ Checkpoint H

1 Add -able to peace .... and service ....
2 Add -ing to frolic .... and mimic ....
3 Add -ous to outrage .... and advantage ....

Activities 1–5

1 Add the endings to the words in brackets making any necessary changes.

Dear Sue,

    I'm (write+ing) .... to you, (hop+ing) .... mad at
the (run+ing) .... battle I've been (have+ing) with Jo.

    We'd (plan+ed) .... a (shop+ing) .... trip together.
I'd been (hope+ing) .... for some (swim+ing) .... and
(dive+ing) .... at the seaside this summer. I'd been
(save+ing) .... up for ages and I'd just
(spot+ed) .... a gorgeous swimsuit in the store and was
thinking of (take+ing) .... it to the (fit+ing) ....
room when, would you believe it, Jo (snap+ed) .... it
from under my nose, (drag+ing) .... it to the check-out
before I could do anything about it.

    (Hope+ing) .... your shoulder is (improve+ing) ....
    Love,

        Di.

    PS I'll be (come+ing) .... to the disco on Friday.

2 Anagrams containing **ie** or **ei**. Write the correct words in the blanks.
  a EHFIC (main) C _ _ _ _
  b VEECAHI (reach, attain) A _ _ _ _ _ _
  c EEVIDCE (mislead or trick) D _ _ _ _ _ _
  d GISEBEE (surround a castle) B _ _ _ _ _ _
  e EGIRN (rule like a king) R _ _ _ _
  f LEVIBEE (think something is true) B _ _ _ _ _ _
  g VISNGOEER (king or queen) S _ _ _ _ _ _ _ _
  h GENIH (make the noise of a horse) N _ _ _ _
  i DILEY (give way) Y _ _ _ _

3 Fill in the blanks.

  a Smok...... is damag...... to your health.
  b No picnic...... on tarmac......d area.
  c Th......ves in ser......s (set) of vic......s attacks.
  d Customers will rec......ve a wri......n g......arantee.
  e Gang g......lty of drug-traffic......g s......ze (grab) for....gners.

4 Fill in the gaps.
The children were all shr......king and argu......ng as they open......d their presents, none of them car......ng where they threw the wrap......ngs, some admir....ng their fr......nds' gifts, some interfer......ng in a fit of misch......f, others hardly disg......sing their disappointment at rec......ving yet another box of handkerch....fs.
It was all very intrig......ng and fatig......ng.

5 Put **ie** or **ei** in the following and then sort them into groups under the headings given below.

  a v _ _ l
  b pr _ _ st
  c l _ _ sure
  d dec _ _ tful
  e rel _ _ ve

  f perc _ _ ve
  g s _ _ ze
  h bel _ _ ve
  i spec _ _ s
  j rec _ _ ve

'ee' sound but not after c	'ee' sound after c	not 'ee' sound	exceptions
chief	ceiling	sleigh	weird
....	....	....	....
....	....	....	....
....	....	....	....

SKILLCHECK Check these statements to assess what you have learned from this chapter. If you cannot honestly tick every statement, go back over the relevant section of the chapter.

❏ I know the difference between long and short vowels and can use this to help with spelling.

❏ I know when to drop the silent 'e' at the end of words and when to keep it.

❏ I know when to double the consonant before -ing or -ed at the end of a word.

❏ I can identify the stress in a word and how to use this to help with spelling.

❏ I know when it's 'ie' and when it's 'ei'.

❏ I know the difference between soft and hard 'c's and 'g's and how this affects spelling.

3

PRONUNCIATION AND SPELLING - DIFFERENCES

- As you'll have noticed, pronunciation and spelling are not always in line with each other. This is partly because English contains many words borrowed from other languages like Old English, French, Latin and Greek. The spelling systems of all these languages are different from one another. Pronunciation and spelling have also changed over the centuries.
- Look at and pronounce these words:
  knight   damn   through   gnarled   character   undoubtedly   solemn   thorough   receipt   knot   physics   manoeuvre
- No wonder many people think there's neither rhyme nor reason to English spelling!

HISTORY AND WORD ORIGINS

In fact, there are often good historical reasons for these oddities. For instance, the 'k' and 'gh' in knight were originally pronounced. Words like character, chaos and chronic, and physical, phobia and psychology come from the Greek. Words with 'gu' come from the French, for example, guide, fatigue and intrigue. They are pronounced with a hard 'g' sound as in goat.

If you look up the origin of a word in a big dictionary, you will often see that the spelling is determined by the language the word comes from. (See Chapter 4, *Using a dictionary*, for more on this and also for a list of the different spellings of certain sounds. See also Chapter 5, *Word families*.)

SILENT LETTERS

There are groups or families of words which share the same origin. One way to help with the spelling of words with 'silent letters' is to consider the sense of the word and think of other words in the same family, for example:

- the silent 'b' in de**b**t: compare debit – from debitum (Latin); also in dou**b**t: undou**b**tedly – from dubitum (Latin) (compare indubitably).
- the silent 'n' after 'm' in autum**n**: compare autumnal where you can hear the 'n'. Similar examples are:
  condemn → condemnation   column → columnar
  damn → damnation   solemn → solemnity
- the silent 'h' in honour, honest, heir is of French origin. (In French the 'h' is never pronounced.)
- 'gn' and 'kn' come from Old English and could originally be heard. Try saying the following with the 'g' and 'k' sounds pronounced:
  The **g**nat **g**nawed at the **g**narled and **k**notted **k**nuckles of the old **g**nu.
- The silent 'p' in cupboard makes sense if you realise it's a board for cups. The 'p' in receipt comes from the Latin root which is also in reception and receptacle.
- The silent 'al': the word accidentally is formed by adding -ly to accident**al**. Other examples are occasion**ally**, incident**ally**.
- The silent 'e':
  veg**e**table → veg**e**tarian   temp**e**rature **but** hot temp**e**r
  lit**e**rature → lit**e**rary
  Say these, stressing the bold letter:
  int**e**rested   desp**e**rate

✓ *Checkpoint A*

Pick out the silent, or almost silent, letters in these. Underline them and overstress them as you say them:
1 chocolate   6 Wednesday
2 surprise   7 chestnut
3 arctic   8 fasten
4 twelfth   9 subtle
5 February

MISPRONUNCIATION

Spelling errors can also be caused by mispronunciation.
  Say these words:
  burglar   mischievous
  intellectual   grievous
  disintegrate   secretary
  undoubtedly   recognise

IT'S UNDOU**B**TEDLY ED

Note that:

- there's no 'u' after the 'g' in burglar
- there's no 'i' after the 'v' in mischievous
- there's no 'r' after the first 'e' in intellectual
- there's no 'i' after the 'v' in grievous
- there's no 'r' after the first 'e' in disintegrate
- it's sec–ret–ary (not 'seckertary')
- it's undoubt**ed**ly (not 'undoubtably')
- it's re**cog**nise (or -ize) (not 'recker ...' or 'reckon ...')
- there's no extra sound after the ath- in athletics and the arth- in arthritis, nor after the hund- in hundred.
- asphalt isn't pronounced ash- but assf- and statistics doesn't begin stast-. Words like these and anemone are easier if you say them slowly.

BREAKING WORDS UP INTO SYLLABLES OR PARTS

Longer words often become slurred or seem difficult because of their length. Break them up and underline the problem area, then they'll become easier:

lab–_or_–a–_to_ry   con–temp_or_–ary   un–_nec_–ess–ary
sec–_ret_–ary   vet–_er_–in–_ary_   it–in–_er_–ary

THE 'UH' SOUND

Vowels are often pronounced with a neutral, or 'uh' sound. The best way to cope with such words is to overstress these vowels when you say them to yourself:

develop   quality   hologram   grammar   admiration (compare admire)   desperate   pencil   escalator   memorable (compare memory)   certain

IS IT 'C' OR 'S'?

How do we know which letter to use? If you listen to the sound of 'a piece of advice' and 'to advise', you should hear a difference which will remind you that the noun has a 'c' and the verb has an 's'. Other examples of c/s:

a practice   a licence   a prophecy (rhymes with see)
to practise   to license   to prophesy (rhymes with eye)

(See also Chapter 9 for endings like -ence/-ense.)

✓ Checkpoint B

Fill in the blanks.
1 The judge sol......mnly conde......ed the prim......tive behaviour of the accused, who was charged with gr......v......s bodily harm.
2 You don't have to be an inte......ectual to enjoy the lux......ry of a lib......ry of good books.
3 Mat......matics ......volves ari......metic and st......istics.
4 The bark of the tree was ......arled and ......otted like the ......uckles of an old man's hand.
5 He was part......c......ly int......ested in the lit......ture of the last cent......ry.
6 It's gen......lly rec......ised (known) that genius ......nvolves ninety per cent persp......ration and ten per cent insp......ration. It cert......nly ......spires adm......ration.
7 She gave the p......lice a d......scription of the burg......r and showed them the broken window fas......nings.
8 It was und......t......ly (certainly) a misch......v......s atte......t (try) to avoid paying his de......ts (what he owed).
9 The choc......ate bar was a su......le (delicate) blend of coc......, coc......nut and veg......ble oil.
10 Parl......ment is the environ......ent of gover......ent, the place where politi......ns take d......ci......ns that ......ffect those living in the...... (belonging to them) constit......cies.
11 It was either We......day the e......th (8th) or Sunday the twel......th of Feb......ary.
12 The ar......tic temp......ratures in the aut...... (after summer) had a disastrous ......ffect on my veg......ables.

1 Fill in the gaps in this letter:

> Dear Sir,
>
> I have read your advertisement in the Lawyers' Gazette for a sec......tary and should be most gr......ful if you would consider me for the post.
>
> I am famili...r with most aspects of ......formation te......nology and have had ei......teen years' bu......ness experi......nce. I am int......ested in legal matters and would welcome the opp......tunity to work in a solicit......r's office.
>
> I enclose my c.v. and the names and ad......esses of two referees.
>
> Yours sinc......ly,
>
> *Lucy Burns*

2 Insert the missing letters in these where necessary:

   a *Police report on bag found in cloakroom*
   brown bag with broken fas_ _ning containing: han_kerchief, pre-pack _ _ san_wiches, small packet of asp_rins, bar of choc_late, bottle of veg_table oil, wallet with di-mond ring, various recei_ts and pi_ture of fam_ly.

   b *Research notes on Bhutan*
   Ar_tic temp_ _tures November till Feb_ _ary, according to Mete_rological Office _ _formation. Northern mount_ _n range _nhabited by yaks and shep_erds and gen_rally unexplored. Clim_ers on previous exp_ditions gave up ex_austed after ei_ _t (8) sep_rate attem_ _s.

3 Insert all **necessary** letters in these headlines. Be careful not to add extra letters or mispronounce words.

   a BURG....R STEALS HUND....D (100) UMB....ELLAS BUT NOT JEW....RY

   b FORMER ATH....ETICS STAR SCORES EIG....H (8TH) CENT....RY

   c COUNTRY'S TOP INTE....LECTUAL PREDICTS DISINTE....RATION OF SOCIETY

   d LOSS OF VITAL EQUIP....ENT HALTS AR....TIC EXP....DITION

4 Add the missing letters in the following:

   a *Music Review*:
   More Persp_ration than Insp_ration
   Rick Starr's eig_ _h concert at Wembley was defin_tely not his best. It was hard to reco_nise in the prim_tive strumming of his ex_austed playing the usually su_tle r_ythms of his solo guitar. At times his act even deteri_rated into r_diculous pantomi_e as he gyrated about the stage making desp_rate attemp_s to _nvolve his audience in clapping routines.

b *Book blurb*

Children b_ _lding san_ castles p_rsued (chased) by giant phantom ane_ones. 'G_ost (phantom) I_land' (land surrounded by water) is action-pack_ _ with ex_ _ting su_prises and mem_rable d_scriptions of the many-tent_cled monsters. This is undou_t_ _ly the most int_ _esting newcomer to children's lit_rature.

c *Preview of TV show:*
The Man in the House

Pro_ably (most likely) our premier feminist sat_rist once again proves laughter the best med_cine, showing up hypocr_ _y and chauv_ _ism in this punchy par_dy (send-up) of male parl_ _mentary priv_l_ge and old-fash_ _ned attitudes.

5 Break all the longer words in the spelling tips below into syllables or parts and then underline the difficult letters, for example, veterinary → vet-**er**-**in**-ary:

a Watch the endings of words like **monastery** .... , **cemetery** .... , **estuary** .... , **similarly** .... , **category** .... , **gradually** .... , **democracy** .... and **hypocrisy** ....

b Break long words up into bits, for instance, **deteriorate** .... , **psychology** .... , **itinerary** .... , **particularly** .... , and **contemporary** .... Say them slowly, and then even words like **unnecessarily** .... , won't seem so **extraordinarily** .... difficult.

c Overstressing the **pronunciation** .... of awkward letters can also be **advantageous** .... Such **techniques** .... help avoid the **embarrassment** .... , of spelling mistakes.

6 Find six words, each with a different pronunciation of 'ough' in it.

SKILLCHECK Check these statements to assess what you have learned from this chapter. If you cannot honestly tick all of these statements, then go back over the relevant section of the chapter.

❏ I know how to look for 'lost letters' and can use this to help with spelling.

❏ I know how using the syllables in words can help to work out the spelling.

❏ I know how to use pronunciation to identify when to use 'c' and when to use 's'.

4
USING A
DICTIONARY

- A good dictionary not only shows you how to spell a word but also:
  - how to pronounce it
  - how to break it into syllables
  - its various meanings and uses
  - what part or parts of speech (for example, noun, adjective, verb) it can be
  - the other forms of the word (like plurals and verb-endings)
  - other words in the same family (to help with spelling and sense)
  - the origin (root and language) of the word (only in the more expensive dictionaries).

  All these are linked to the spelling and help explain it.

- A good dictionary is essential for all users of English. It's best to have more than one – a pocket edition and a large one. Choose carefully, checking the publication date at the front to make sure you're buying the latest edition.

- Ask yourself if it gives you a clear pronunciation guide. Look at the explanation of symbols and abbreviations in the introduction. Dictionaries that give the origin of a word can be useful because this often makes sense of the spelling.

FINDING A WORD

This isn't as easy as it sounds. You could spend some time looking under 's' for psychology.

Obviously words will be arranged alphabetically. Use the guide words at the top of the page to speed up the search.

Remember that some sounds can be represented by different letters:

■ CONSONANT SOUND	LETTER(S) USED
k	c (collapse) k (keenness) ch (chaos)
f	f (friend) ph (physics)
g (as in goat)	g (gardener) gh (ghastly) gu (guarded)
j	j (jealous) ge (general) gi (giant)
n	n (noticeable) kn (knowledge) gn (gnarled) pn (pneumonia) mn (mnemonic)
r	r (religious) rh (rhythm)
s	s (sentence) c (ceiling) sc (scissors, scene) ps (psychology)
sh	sh (shield) sch (schedule) ch (chateau)
sk	sk (skilful) sch (scheme, school) sc (scare)
t	t (truly) Th (Thames) pt (pterodactyl)
w	w (weather) wh (whether meaning if)
z	z (zenith) x (xylophone) cz (czar)

4

■ VOWEL SOUND	CAN BE SPELT
ee (as in bee)	ee (meet) ea (meat) ie (chief) ei (seize) e + consonant + e (scene) ae (aegis)
ay (as in say)	a + consonant + e (lane) ai (daily) ey (prey) ay (pray) eigh (neighbours) ei (vein)
air	ear (pear) a + consonant + e (share) air (fair) eir (heir) aer (aerodrome)
aw (as in paw)	or (sore) aw (gnaw) au (audit) augh (taught) ough (noughts)
ear	ere (here) ear (hear) ier (cavalier) eer (sheer)
oh (as in snow)	oa (oak) o + consonant + e (alone) ow (snow) ough (though)
ah (as in father)	a (father) ar (cart) al (calm)
I (eye)	i (pine) is (island) ig (sign) eigh (height) igh (high) ie (fiery) i + consonant + e (site)
yoo	ue (barbecue) eue (queue) ew (few) eu (feud) u (cucumber)

And the 'uh' sound could be almost any vowel or combination of vowels.

Make a card of these for use as a bookmark and keep it in your dictionary.
    (If you really can't find the word, ask someone for the first three letters, but don't get out of the habit of looking words up for yourself.)

PRONUNCIATION

A good dictionary will give the pronunciation of the word, including how to break it up into syllables. It will also show where the stress is. (See also Chapters 3 and 7.)

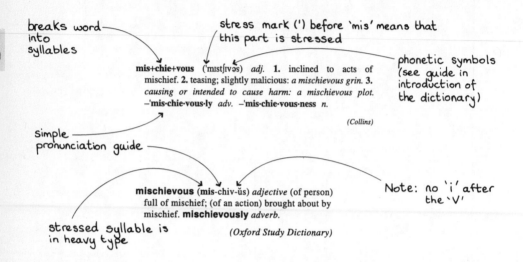

breaks word into syllables

stress mark (') before 'mis' means that this part is stressed

mis+chie+vous ('mɪstʃɪvəs) *adj.* **1.** inclined to acts of mischief. **2.** teasing; slightly malicious: *a mischievous grin.* **3.** *causing or intended to cause harm: a mischievous plot.* –'**mis·chie·vous·ly** *adv.* –'**mis·chie·vous·ness** *n.*

phonetic symbols (see guide in introduction of the dictionary)

(Collins)

simple pronunciation guide

mischievous (mis-chiv-ūs) *adjective* (of person) full of mischief; (of an action) brought about by mischief. **mischievously** *adverb.*

Note: no 'i' after the 'v'

stressed syllable is in heavy type

(Oxford Study Dictionary)

Larger dictionaries use a special pronunciation alphabet called the phonetic alphabet. (It's worth getting to know these symbols, but you can also check the pronunciation in a smaller dictionary.)

Look up the spelling and pronunciation of the word pro**nun**ciation: as you'll see, it's got -nun- in the middle, not -noun- like pronounce. Work out how to pronounce indictment, renege and exacerbate, using more than one dictionary if necessary. You'll need to study the key to pronunciation in the dictionary's introduction as different systems and symbols are used. Some dictionaries, for instance, show the stress by putting a mark **before** the stressed sound; others put the stressed sound in heavy type, for example, '**instance, i**nstance.

The stress can determine the spelling. Admitted has two 't's because the stress is at the **end** of ad**mit**. Orbited and offered have one 't' and 'r' because the stress is not at the end in **or**bit and **off**er. (See Chapter 7.)

✓ Checkpoint A

Look up these words in a good dictionary. Find the stress, then add **-ed**, for example, orbit → **or**bited:

1 cosset ....
2 benefit ....
3 defer ....
4 rivet ....

5 plummet ....
6 prefer ....
7 commit ....

Mispronunciation can also cause misspelling. Again, the dictionary helps.
Find out what's wrong with these by looking them up. Check the
pronunciation, too:

   asprin   diptheria   categry   umberella   atheletics

PARTS OF SPEECH

The dictionary also tells you what job(s) of work the word does or, in other
words, what part of speech it is or can be (for example, noun, verb,
adjective). (See *Terms you need to know*, in the Introduction.)

   Sometimes this is important for the spelling of a word. The words practi**ce**,
licen**ce** and advi**ce** are all nouns, while practi**se**, licen**se** and advi**se** are
verbs. If you look up prophe**cy** (noun) and prophe**sy** (verb), you will see that
they are also pronounced differently. The word separate can be a verb (to
separ**a**te) or an adjective (pronounced **sep**ret). Both are spelt sep**arat**e.

WORD FORMS AND FAMILIES

Study these dictionary entries for 'prefer' and its family:

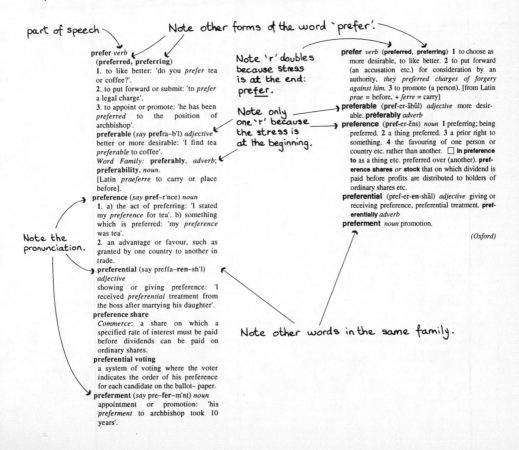

part of speech

Note other forms of the word `prefer'.

prefer *verb*
(**preferred, preferring**)
1. to like better: 'do you *prefer* tea
or coffee?'.
2. to put forward or submit: 'to *prefer*
a legal charge'.
3. to appoint or promote: 'he has been
preferred to the position of
archbishop'.
preferable (*say* prefra–b'l) *adjective*
better or more desirable: 'I find tea
preferable to coffee'.
Word Family: **preferably**, *adverb*;
preferability, *noun*.
[Latin *praeferre* to carry or place
before].

Note 'r' doubles
because stress
is at the end:
pre*fer*.

Note only
one `r' because
the stress is
at the beginning.

prefer *verb* (**preferred, preferring**) 1 to choose as
more desirable, to like better. 2 to put forward
(an accusation etc.) for consideration by an
authority, *they preferred charges of forgery
against him.* 3 to promote (a person). [from Latin
prae = before, + *ferre* = carry]
preferable (pref-er-ăbŭl) *adjective* more desirable. **preferably** *adverb*
preference (pref-er-ĕns) *noun* 1 preferring; being
preferred. 2 a thing preferred. 3 a prior right to
something. 4 the favouring of one person or
country etc. rather than another. ☐ **in preference
to** as a thing etc. preferred over (another). **preference shares** *or* **stock** that on which dividend is
paid before profits are distributed to holders of
ordinary shares etc.
preferential (pref-er-en-shăl) *adjective* giving or
receiving preference, preferential treatment. **pref-
erentially** *adverb*
preferment *noun* promotion.

(*Oxford*)

preference (*say* pref–r'nce) *noun*
1. a) the act of preferring: 'I stated
my *preference* for tea'. b) something
which is preferred: 'my *preference*
was tea'.
2. an advantage or favour, such as
granted by one country to another in
trade.

Note the
pronunciation.

preferential (*say* preffa–**ren**–sh'l)
adjective
showing or giving preference: 'I
received *preferential* treatment from
the boss after marrying his daughter'.
preference share
Commerce: a share on which a
specified rate of interest must be paid
before dividends can be paid on
ordinary shares.
preferential voting
a system of voting where the voter
indicates the order of his preference
for each candidate on the ballot–paper.
preferment (*say* pre–**fer**–m'nt) *noun*
appointment or promotion: 'his
preferment to archbishop took 10
years'.

Note other words in the same family.

Many dictionaries give the other forms of a word like its verb endings and tenses, and plurals.

By studying the origin of the word (given here in brackets at the end) you can see that these words are in the same family. This helps with spelling as you can use your knowledge of one word, for instance the word medical, to spell another, like medicine.

In bigger dictionaries the origin of the word (i.e. its root and the word and language the word originates from) will be given, usually at the end of the entry.

Study these entries for the word 'conscious':

con+scious (kɒnʃəs) adj. 1. a. denoting or relating to a part of the human mind that is aware of a person's self, environment, and mental activity and that to a certain extent determines his choices of action. b. (as n.): the conscious is only a small part of the mind. 2. alert and awake; not sleeping or comatose. 3. a. aware of a particular fact or phenomenon: I am conscious of your great kindness to me. b. (in combination): clothes-conscious. ~Compare unconscious. [C17: from Latin conscius sharing knowledge, from com-with + scīre to know] —'con+scious+ly adv. —'con+scious+ness n.

(Collins)

'conscious/'konshəs/ adj 1 perceiving with a degree of controlled thought or observation 2 personally felt 3 capable of or marked by thought, will, intention, or perception 4 having mental faculties undulled by sleep, faintness, or stupor; awake 5 done or acting with critical awareness <made a ~effort to avoid the same mistakes> 6 marked by awareness of or concern for sthg specified , <a fashion-conscious shopper> [L conscius, fr com- + scire to know] - consciously adv

(Longman's Concise)

Note the 'sci' in the root (also in conscience, science, etc.

And look at the origin of the word 'biscuit':

bis+cuit ('bɪskɪt) n. 1. Brit. a small flat dry sweet or plain cake of many varieties, baked from a dough. U.S. word: cookie. 2. U.S. a kind of small roll similar to a muffin. 3. a. a pale brown or yellowish-grey colour. b. (as adj.): biscuit gloves. 4. Also called: bisque. earthenware or porcelain that has been fired but not glazed, 5. take the biscuit. Brit. to be regarded (by the speaker) as the most surprising thing that could have occurred. [C14: from Old French, from (pain) bescuit twice-cooked (bread), from bes BIS + cuire to cook, from Latin coquere]

(Collins)

Note that the origin makes sense of the spelling: bis (twice) + cuit (cooked).

✓ Checkpoint C

Look up the origin of these words:

1 mortgage
2 lieutenant
3 chauvinist
4 democracy
5 immigrant
6 permanent
7 geography
8 festival

You'll soon find that you'll begin to recognise which language a word comes from. Words with 'rh', 'ph', 'ps' and 'ch' (when pronounced as 'k') come from Greek; words with 'gn', 'kn', 'wh' and a silent 'gh' come from Old English, whereas words ending in -eur, -ance and with a 'gu' are often from French.

• REMEMBER: make constant use of your dictionary.

Activities 1–3

1 These words have been written as they are said. See if you can find them in your dictionary. Use the guide in *Finding the Word*, above.

  a 'kertyus' (polite) ....
  b 'sherard' (absurd act or show) ....
  c 'skitsafrenik' (with a split mind) ....
  d 'syoodonim' (false name) ....
  e 'sifer' (secret writing) ....
  f 'showvinizm' (assuming your own sex, race or nation is best) ....
  g 'karizma' (special power of personality) ....
  h 'tort' (tight) ....
  i 'nollidge' (information) ....
  j 'sarm' (hymn) ....
  k 'ile' (gangway, for example, in a church) ....

2 Detective work on roots and origins.
  Use a big dictionary to find out the origin – and think about the spelling – of these words. (Example: biscuit, from French 'bis', meaning twice + 'cuit' meaning cooked.

     surprise   maintenance   Wednesday   February   grateful
     Mediterranean   desiccated

3 Read the following holiday centre advertisement and see if you can tell which language each of the words in bold type comes from. Then check each word's origin in a dictionary.

THE BLUE WAVES HOLIDAY EXPERIENCE!

Holidays for all the family – chaos or bliss? Choose the easy way at the Blue Waves Family Holiday Centre where there's something for every age and interest.

Fancy a spot of **yacht**ing on the **reservoir**? Or do you prefer some peaceful angling from the **wharf**, savouring the **beauty** of our coastal **scenery** and the gentle **rhythm** of the waves? You can try almost any watersport – and there's no need to bring heaps of **paraphernalia** – we'll provide the equipment as well as instruction of the highest standard.

And what about the children? We guarantee they'll enjoy themselves – no more **whinges**, no more **awkward** arrangements to make as you struggle to suit everybody – just **liaise** with our qualified staff and they'll provide all the **surveillance** and company your children need. And there's plenty for them to do! They can develop their **techniques** in a whole range of games and sports – maybe trying a few **manoeuvres** on the go-kart **circuit** (also popular with parents)!

Child supervision is also available in the evenings, so that **connoisseurs** can enjoy the delights of the **Blue Waves Bistro and Restaurant.**

We're sure the **consensus** will be: the best family holiday ever!

SKILLCHECK   Check these statements to assess what you have learned from this chapter. If you cannot honestly tick all of these statements, then go back over the relevant section of the chapter.

❑ I know the different ways in which certain sounds can be spelled, and can use this to help with finding words in a dictionary.

❑ I can use a dictionary to identify the stress in a word.

❑ I can use a dictionary to identify word families.

❑ I can use a dictionary to identify parts of speech.

5
WORD
FAMILIES

- You'll need a dictionary for this chapter.
- Words often belong to families that have the same 'roots'.

  What do the words in each of these groups have in common?

  1 finish   definition   definitely   indefinite   infinitesimal
  2 signature   assign   signal   designer   assignation
    insignia   assignment
  3 conscious   science   conscientious   subconsciously
    conscience   unscientifically

- The words in group 1 all come from the Latin word 'finire' meaning 'to end'. That is why all these words are spelt with a 'fini' in them.
- Now look at the root in groups 2 and 3 above. The key letters in group 2 are 'sign' from the Latin word 'signum' meaning a 'mark'. In group 3 they are 'sci' from the Latin 'scire' to know. This makes sense of the spelling of words like conscious, conscientious and assignment.

MORE ABOUT ROOTS

Here are a few more roots found in commonly misspelt words:

- 'rid' (Latin ridere meaning to laugh):   **rid**iculous   de**rid**e
- 'para' (Latin parare meaning to set or get):   se**par**ate   pre**par**ation
  The word separate is made up from 'se', meaning apart, and the root 'para', meaning set – hence separate (set apart).
- 'scend' (climb):   de**scend** (climb down)   a**scend**
- 'cite' (stir up):   in**cite**   ex**cite**
- 'cogn' (get to know):   re**cogn**ise   in**cogn**ito
- 'rupt' (tear, break):   **rupt**ure   inter**rupt**
- 'hibit' (hold, have):   in**hibit** (hold in)   ex**hibit**ion

Sometimes the root has more than one form:

- 'scribe' and 'script' (write): describe   prescription
- 'ceive', 'cip', 'cept' (take): except (taken out)   receive   recipient receptive
- 'mit', 'miss' (send): commit   mission   dismiss

For each of the three groups of roots given above, find at least eight more examples of related words. Use the prefix list in this chapter to help you.

USING RELATED WORDS TO FIND THE RIGHT SPELLING

Do you have trouble spelling any of these?

medicine   privilege   prejudice   government   library   condemn solemn?

It helps to think of words in the same family where the spelling is easier. Med**ic**al reminds you of the 'i' after the 'd' in medicine. **Cent**ral is in the same family as con**cent**rate; **jud**icial and pre**jud**ice have a common root. So do **norm**al and e**norm**ous.

When the vowel sound has become slurred, think of another word in the same family where the letter is clearly pronounced, for example:

lib**ra**ry → lib**ra**rian   gramm**a**r → gramm**a**tical
condem**n** → condem**n**ation   solem**n** → solem**n**ity   mus**c**le → mus**c**ular
gove**rn** → gove**rn**ment   re**a**l → re**a**lity   crit**ic** → crit**ic**ise
categ**o**ry → categ**o**rical

PREFIXES

A prefix is a group of letters or a letter added to the front of a word or root. The word prefix, for instance, is made up from the base word fix and the prefix **pre-** meaning in front.

To find words in a dictionary and to explore their roots and families you'll need a list of the commonest prefixes.

With the help of this list and a good dictionary you will be able to build up word families and link up the spelling of words. You will also be able to connect the meaning, the origin and the spelling of words and widen your vocabulary.

LIST OF COMMON PREFIXES

Prefix	Examples
a, ab, abs (from, away)	*avert abhorrent abstain*
ad (to, towards)	*advertisement adhere*
ante (before)	*ante-room antedate*
anti (against)	*antiseptic antibiotics*
bi, bis (two, twice)	*bicycle bisexual biscuit*
circum (round)	*circumference circumvent*
co, con (together, with)	*co-operate contemporary*
contra, contro (against)	*contradict controversial*
de (down, away from)	*descend denationalise*
dis (not, apart)	*disappear disservice*
e, ex (out of)	*eject exit*
extra (outside, beyond)	*extraordinary extraterrestrial*
for (not)	*forbidden forgo (go without)*
fore (before)	*forecast forecourt*
hyper (over, beyond, in excess)	*hypertension hypersensitive*
hypo (under)	*hypodermic hypothermia*
in (not or into)	*inaudible invade*
inter (between, among)	*interrupt intervene*
intro (within)	*introduce introverted*
mis (not, wrongly)	*misspell mistake*
ob (in the way)	*obstruction obstacle*
per (through)	*pervasive peruse*
peri (around)	*periscope perimeter*
post (after)	*postpone postscript*
pre (before, in front)	*precede premature*
pro (onwards)	*progress proceed*
re (back, again)	*return recurring*
se (apart)	*separate segregate*
sub (under)	*submarine subversive*
super (over)	*supervise superintendent*
sur (on, over)	*surprise surmount*
sym, syn (together)	*symphony synthesiser*
tele (far)	*telegraph television*
trans (across)	*transport transmit*
un (not)	*unnecessary unnatural*

5

WORD FAMILIES

ADDING PREFIXES TO WORDS

Normally prefixes are simply added to the base word or root without any spelling changes (but see the next two sections below).

For example, the prefix **dis-** added to appear gives us disappear.
Also: dis- + appoint → disappoint   dis- + approve → disapprove
      dis- + obey → disobey   dis- + service → disservice
      dis- + satisfied → dissatisfied
(Note that a double 's' appears only if the word or root begins with an 's'.)

Here are some other prefixes:
un- + natural → unnatural   **under-** + rate → underrate
mis- + spell → misspell

✓ Checkpoint A

Follow the same pattern to identify the prefix and baseword in these words:

prefix		base word or root		word
over	+	rule	→	overrule
1		....		mislaid
2		....		interrupt
3		....		excite
4		....		withhold
5		....		misshapen
6		....		disagree
7		....		dissimilar
8		....		surround
9		....		surprise
10		....		describe
11		....		descend
12		....		address

PREFIXES WHICH ADAPT

Some prefixes adapt to suit the first letter of the base word or root.

Adding 'ad-'

The prefix **ad-** (meaning to or towards) often changes to suit the first letter of the base word or root. This happens when the base word or root begins with the letters b, c, f, g, l, n, p, r, s and t:

- in arrange **ad-** has changed to 'ar' to suit the 'r' of range
- in attract **ad-** has changed to 'at' to suit the 't' of tract (draw)
- in appear **ad-** has changed to 'ap' to suit the 'p' of pear.

This explains why the following words have double letters near the beginning:

- **abb**reviate (ad + brev – brief)   **acc**laim   **ann**ounce (ad + nounce – give a message)
- **ass**ociate (ad + sociate – join)

Before base words or roots beginning with 'k' and 'q', **ad-** changes to 'ac': acknowledge acquire (ad + quire – get) acquit (ad + quit – free)

✓ *Checkpoint B*

Complete the following:
1 ad + celerate (speed) ....
2 ad + gravate (make worse) ....
3 ad + point ....
4 ad + prove ....
5 ad + rears ....
6 ad + tend ....
7 ad + proach ....

Other adapting prefixes
A similar thing often happens to the prefixes con-, in-, ob- and sub-:

- **con-** (meaning with, together) changes before l, m, p and r, for example, con- becomes 'cor' before respond to make **cor**respond. There is a similar change in collect (con + lect – gather), commemorate (con + memorate – remember) and correct (con + rect – right).
- **in-** (meaning not) often changes before l, m and r, for example, it changes to 'il' in **il**legal, to 'im' in **im**mature and to 'ir' in **ir**regular.
- **ob-** (meaning against or in the way of) changes before 'c' and 'p', for example, it becomes 'oc' in **oc**cur (run in the way) and 'op' in **op**pose (place against).
- **sub-** (meaning under) usually changes before c, f, g, m, p and r, for example, sub- changes to 'suf' in **suf**fer (from Latin ferre meaning to bear, to put up with) and to 'sup' in **sup**press (push under).
- **dis-** often changes before 'f', for example, **dif**ferent, **dif**fuse.

5

WORD FAMILIES

✓ Checkpoint C

Complete the following:
Example: con + lide → collide
1 con + mend → ....
2 con + mit → ....
3 con + rupt → ....
4 in + mortal → ....
5 in + relevant → ....
6 in + responsible → ....
7 ob + cur → ....
8 ob + position → ....
9 sub + fix → ....
10 sub + press → ....
11 sub + pose → ....

Prefixes ending in 'l'

- The word **all** when used as a prefix drops one 'l':   almighty   almost altogether   alright
- Similarly with **well**:   welcome   welfare

DON'T MIX UP THESE PREFIXES:

- **ante-** (before): ante-room   antecedent
  anti- (against): antiseptic   antidote
- **for-** (not): forbid forsake
  fore- (before, in front):   forecast   forecourt
- **hyper-** (beyond, over):   hyperactive
  hypo- (under):   hypodermic (under the skin)   hypothermia (under normal levels of heat)
- **pre-** (before):   predict   precede (go in front or before)
  pro- (along):   progress   proceed (go along)

ADDING PREFIXES TO 'CEED' AND 'CEDE'

The root **ceed** or **cede** means 'to go' and combines with a large number of prefixes.
A rhyme helps:

With suc-, ex- and pro-
Double 'e' must go.

So it's succeed, exceed, proceed (but procedure).
Otherwise it's 'cede': recede, precede, intercede, accede.
Supersede, however, has an 's' because it comes from another root (from Latin sedere meaning to sit).

1 Star-formations. Use your dictionary and the list of prefixes for this. Find as many words as you can belonging to the same family, using these roots:

  a loqu/locut (speak)
  b pone/pose/posit (place, put)
  c vers/vert (turn)
  d voc/vok (voice, call)
  e dic/dict (say)

Set them out in star-formation like this:

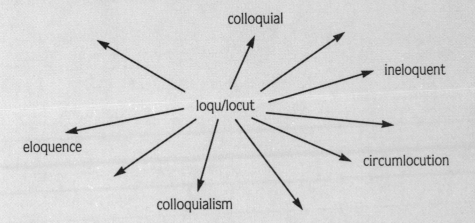

2 Find as many words as you can containing these roots:

  a phon (sound)
  b cracy (government)
  c chron (time)
  d psych (mind)
  e scen (stage)
  f graph (writing)

3 Look up the origin of these in a dictionary:
mortgage grateful Mediterranean maintenance Wednesday ecstasy
desiccated manoeuvre

4 Fill in the missing letter. Finding a companion word will help, for example,
ad–ration → adore.

  a adm–ration
  b gr–teful
  c defin–te
  d persp–ration
  e mem–rable
  f auth–r
  g exp–dition

5

WORD FAMILIES

5 What's wrong here?

  a Anti-natal care (Notice on a doctor's surgery)
  b Frozen stiff and suffering from hyperthermia
  c I was preceding along the road.
  d Billy the Kid was prescribed as an outlaw.

6 Correct these notices:

ROOMS ALOCATED   AQUIRE A BODY-BEAUTIFUL   USE DOOR OPOSITE
FORTUNES FORCAST   PERMISSION WITHELD

7 Make negatives by adding prefixes to these, for example, legible→illegible:

  a logical ....
  b regular ....
  c responsible ....
  d mobile ....
  e natural ....
  f reversible ....
  g noble ....
  h necessary ....

8 Wordsearch. Find twelve words each containing a prefix. There are no diagonals.

W	L	R	T	I	M	M	O	C
I	Q	N	P	B	U	F	V	R
T	E	S	U	F	E	R	E	D
H	E	U	R	E	X	E	R	T
H	S	R	R	J	C	T	R	E
O	P	P	O	S	E	N	U	V
L	A	R	C	M	P	Y	L	N
D	L	I	X	E	T	Z	E	L
B	E	S	O	P	P	U	S	G
N	R	E	S	I	G	N	E	D

9 Add the prefixes **ad-**, **con-**, **ob-** or **sub-** to the following base words or roots (some can form more than one new word):

prefix	base word or root	word
ad	company	accompany
....	grieve	....
....	lapse (fall)	....
....	press	....
....	point	....
....	quit (free)	....
....	rect (right)	....
....	pose	....
....	nounce (give a message)	....
....	proximate (near)	....
....	custom	....
....	gravate (make worse)	....
....	nihilate (make nothing)	....
....	cur (run, happen)	....
....	casion (fall, happen)	....

SKILLCHECK   Check these statements to assess what you have learned from this chapter. If you cannot honestly tick all of these statements, then go back over the relevant section of the chapter.

❑ I know how to use the meanings of roots and prefixes to help with spelling.

❑ I know how to add prefixes to words correctly.

6

ADDING ENDINGS TO WORDS

- **An ending or a suffix is a part of a word added to the end of a base word or root, for example, the suffixes -ful and -ness as in careful and suddenness.**
- **A suffix which begins with a consonant is called a CONSONANT-suffix.**

ADDING CONSONANT-SUFFIXES

Do you know why careless and excitement keep the 'e', while caring and exciting don't?

And why do beauty and happy change to beautiful and happiness when marrying and supplying don't change?

Generally, when you add a **consonant**-suffix to any root or word (except those ending in 'y'), you simply put the two together without any changes:

> govern + ment → government   excite + ment → excitement
> keen + ness → keenness   stubborn + ness → stubbornness
> care + ful → careful   hope + less → hopeless
> sad + ness → sadness   amaze + ment → amazement

Main exceptions: argument   awful

(See Chapter 8, *Adverbs* for adding -ly.)

But this rule does **not** apply when adding to words ending in 'y', **nor** does it apply to VOWEL-suffixes (suffixes that begin with a vowel).
(See Chapter 7.)

6

Complete these by adding **-ment**, **-ful**, **-less** or **-ness**:
1 manage ....
2 barren ....
3 event ....
4 clue ....
5 advertise ....
6 woe ....
7 develop ....
8 entice ....

CHANGING 'Y' TO 'I'

What happens when

• an 's' is added to journey and supply
• -ed is added to convey and marry
• -ing is added to enjoy and reply
• -ment is added to merry?

The next two rules show when 'y' remains and when it changes to 'i'.

> **RULE** For words ending in a VOWEL + Y, especially -ey (for example, journey) just add the suffix:
> journey → journeys, journeying, journeyed

Also: convey → conveying, conveyed, conveyance
deploy → deploying, deployed, deployment

Exceptions: SAY → SAID LAY → LAID (and mislaid) PAY → PAID
(and repaid, but repayment) DAY → DAILY GAY → GAILY – nearly all
common, one-syllabled words

1 Add -s, -ed and -ment to enjoy ....
2 Add -s, -ing and -ed to survey ....
3 Add -s, -ed and -ing to volley ....

> **RULE** If the word ends in a CONSONANT + Y, change the Y to I when adding **any** suffix **except** -ING:
> happy → happier, happiest, happiness
> marry → marries, married, marriage **but** marrying

Here are a few more examples:

- merry → merriest, merrily, merriment
- pity → pities, pitied, pitiful, pitiless **but** pitying
- busy → busier, busiest, business (trade) **but** busying (busyness means being busy)
- deny → denial, denies, denied **but** denying
- likely → likelihood
- lonely → loneliness, loneliest
- holy → holiday

Exceptions: shyness dryness slyness wryness shyly (all based on words of one syllable)

✓ Checkpoint C

1 Add -ing and -ed to satisfy ....
2 Add -ing and -ed to envy ....
3 Add -ing and -ed to reply ....
4 Add -hood to lively ....
5 Add -ance to apply ....
6 Add -ness to empty ....

▌ CHANGING 'IE' TO 'Y'

A few short common words change from 'ie' to 'y' before **-ing**:
die (dies, died) **but** dying   tie → tying   lie → lying

THE SILENT 'E'

▌ DROPPING THE SILENT 'E' (See also Chapter 6)

> **RULE** When a VOWEL-suffix (like -ing, -ed) is added to a word ending in a silent 'e', the silent 'e' is dropped:
> stare → staring, stared   hope → hoping, hoped   use → using

Also: forgive → forgiving, forgivable   rescue → rescuing
      manoeuvre → manoeuvring   pursue → pursuing
      No QUEUING   No ARGUING

Note: The silent 'e' is kept when adding **consonant**-suffixes, for example,
      management, excitement, useless

Exceptions: ARGUMENT TRULY DULY WHOLLY

The 'e' is sometimes kept

- in words ending -oe: canoeing, toeing, shoeing, hoeing
- to stress the long vowel: mileage, rateable, saleable
- to avoid confusion: dyeing (colouring), singeing (burning), swingeing
  (huge, as in cuts), re-routeing (diverting)
- when adding -ous and -able to words ending in -ce and -ge, for example,
  noticeable, courageous

■ KEEPING THE SILENT 'E' AFTER 'C' AND 'G'

RULE To keep the 'c' and 'g' soft (like 's' and 'j' sounds) when adding
         suffixes starting with 'o' and 'a' (-ous and -able), the silent 'e' must
         stay:
         notice → noticeable   manage → manageable
         courage → courageous   outrage → outrageous

Contrast the pronunciation of navi**ga**ble and knowled**gea**ble, and of
practi**ca**ble and servi**cea**ble.

✓ *Checkpoint D*

Complete these:
1 Add -ous to advantage ....
2 Add -able to change ....
3 Add -ous to gorge ....

WHEN DOES A 'C' NEED A 'K'?

RULE A 'k' is added after the 'c' when VOWEL-suffixes beginning with 'i'
         and 'e' (like -ing and -er and -ed) are added:
         picnic → picnicking, picnicker, picnicked

Also: panic → panicked   traffic → trafficking, trafficker
      mimic → mimicked   bivouac → bivouacked   tarmac → tarmacked

DROPPING A VOWEL WITHIN WORDS

Sometimes, when we add a suffix, a letter will drop out of the base word:

- the 'u' drops out of words ending in -our when -ous is added:

  humour → hum**o**rous   vigour → vig**o**rous   glamour → glam**o**rous

  HUMOROUS story   GLAMOROUS dress

  Also: generous → generosity   curious → curiosity   labour → laborious

This does not happen when -able is added: honourable   favourable

- Words ending in -er and -or **sometimes** drop the 'e' or 'o':

  hunger → hungry   enter → entrance   disaster → disastrous
  hinder → hindrance

  Exceptions include: boist**e**rous sland**e**rous murd**e**rous murd**e**ress
  adult**e**rous adult**e**ress

- Words ending in -nounce drop the 'o':

  pronounce → pro**nun**ciation   denounce → de**nun**ciation
  announce → an**nun**ciation

- Words ending in -claim drop the 'i':

  exclaim → ex**clam**ation   proclaim → pro**clam**ation
  acclaim → ac**clam**ation

✓ *Checkpoint E*

Complete these:
1 Add -ing to panic .... tie ....
2 Add -ous to adventure .... rigour .... disaster ....
  vapour ....
3 Add -ing to spare .... occupy .... dye .... die ....

CHANGING 'F' TO 'V'

An 'f' changes to 'v' before vowel suffixes:
  grief → grievous   mischief → mischievous   thief → thieving
(To make the plural of words ending in 'f' or 'fe' see page 80.)

1 Fill in the blanks where necessary.

  a All expenses P......D

  b Milk deliveries D......LY

  c No PICNI......ING

  d Better to have TR......D and failed ...

  e CURI......TY killed the cat.

  f Have you LA......D the table?

  g Stop ARGU......ING.

  h She was DY......ING her hair.

  i The LONEL......NESS of the Long Distance Runner

2 Fill in the gaps.

  'There's been a notic......ble improv......ent in bus......ness lately,' s......d Cyril cheer......ly.

  'Can't say I've been notic......ng it,' repl......d Jonah gloom......ly.

  'But more and more customers have been repl......ing, more applicants have appl......ed and more advertisers have suppl......ed revenue. There's no den......ing that, you know, and there's every likel......hood of a further upturn in bus......ness. We could eas......ly have that overdraft p......d off by Christmas.'

  'I suppose I shouldn't be arg......ing but tr......ing harder to get more bus......ness, instead of just l......ing (from lie) here occup......ing myself doing nothing. After all, our livel......hood depends on it.'

  'Funn......ly enough, you could be right,' s......d Cyril, this time not disagre......ng.

3 Mini-scrabble. Put the letters I Y I E I I I Y in the right spaces on the board.

	F			A	B	L	•
	U		P		U		
	N		A		S		T
U	N	T	•	D	•	L	•
	•		D		N		•
	E				E		N
	S				S		G
	T	R	•	•	S		

SKILLCHECK Check these statements to assess what you have
learned from this chapter. If you cannot honestly tick
all of these statements, then go back over the
relevant section of the chapter.

❏ I know what consonant-suffixes are and how to add them to words
correctly.

❏ I know what vowel-suffixes are and how to add them to words correctly.

❏ I know when 'y' changes to 'i'.

❏ I know when 'ie' changes to 'y'.

❏ I know when to drop the silent 'e' when a suffix is added, and when to
keep it.

❏ I know when 'k' needs to be added to a 'c'.

❏ I know when to drop a vowel before adding a suffix.

❏ I know when 'f' changes to 'v'.

7

TO DOUBLE OR NOT TO DOUBLE?

■ **The rules about doubling letters are the most useful of all spelling rules to understand. They affect hundreds of words in constant use.**

WORDS OF **ONE** SYLLABLE ENDING IN A SINGLE SHORT VOWEL AND A CONSONANT

Say these words aloud:

hop   hope   tap   tape

and now these:

hopping   hoping   tapping   taping

The double letter is needed in hopping and tapping to keep the vowel sound 'short' (that, is like the 'o' in hop, not 'long' like the 'o' in hope).

Pronounce these words:

ripping   fitted   wrapper   robber   skipping   swimming   scarred

How would these words be said if they didn't have double letters?

> **RULE**   For one-syllable words **ending in one short vowel + a consonant** – for example, hop, tap – double the final letter before VOWEL-suffixes, but NOT before consonant-suffixes:
> fit + vowel suffixes -ing and -ed → fitting and fitted
> but fit + consonant-suffix -ment → fitment

Compare: sad + vowel suffix -en → sadden with sad + consonant-suffix -ness → sadness.

Further examples of adding vowel-suffixes:

hop → hopping, hopped   tap → tapping, tapped
swim → swimming   grab → grabbing, grabbed

| SWIMMING pool | | STARRING Marlon Brando |

Exception: words ending in 'w', 'x', and 'y': saw → sawed   tax → taxed
try → tried   stay → stayed

This also does not apply to words ending in:

- two vowels and a consonant: heap → heaped   weed → weeded
- two consonants: warn → warned   start → started

✓ Checkpoint A

1 Add -ing to   beg ....   pot ....   put ....   hug ....
2 Add -ed to   drop ....   skin ....   trip ....   spar ....
3 Add -er to   sad ....   rob ....   run ....   wet ....
4 Add -ness to   sad ....   wet ....   fit ....
5 Add -en to   sad ....   hid ....   rot ....

7

TO DOUBLE ...?

LONGER WORDS ENDING IN A SINGLE VOWEL AND A CONSONANT

Look at the endings of these words:

    commit   prefer   happen   target

All of them end in a single vowel followed by a single consonant. What happens when we add suffixes to these words?

- Consonant-suffixes are simply added to the base word:
    commit → commitment   prefer → preferment

    But what happens when we add VOWEL-suffixes like -ing, -ed, -er, -able?

- It all depends where the STRESS is.
    Say these words aloud: admit   refer   commit   prefer
    The stress in all these is on the **last** syllable.
    Now say these:
        orbit   happen   offer   target
    The stress is NOT at the end in these.

> **RULE** If the **stress** is at the **end**, double the last letter before adding
> VOWEL-suffixes. If the stress isn't at the end, don't double:
> admit (stress at the END) → admitted, admitting
> happen (stress not at the end) → happened, happening

▪ TO DOUBLE OR NOT TO DOUBLE?

The stress at the END gives two 't's in COM**MIT**TED.
And the same rule applies to PER**MIT**TED, AD**MIT**TED;
But the stress at the start gives just one 't' in **LIM**ITED
And likewise in **TAR**GETED, **BUDG**ETED, **OR**BITED.

The main exception to this rule is words ending in 'l'.

Examples of words where the stress is at the END:
    occur → occurred, occurring, occurrence
    begin → beginning, beginner
    commit → committed, committing, committee

weather PERMITTING

in the BEGINNING

games COMMITTEE

Examples of words where the stress is NOT at the end:
happen → happened, happening   limit → limited   offer → offered,
offering   gallop → galloped, galloping   abandon → abandoned
alter → altering, alteration   benefit → benefited

No ADMITTANCE

Waiting LIMITED

Bargains OFFERED

What's HAPPENED?

Remember: double **only** if the stress is at the **end**.
Now say these words aloud and see how the spelling and the stress are linked:
    pre**fer** → pre**ferr**ing, pre**ferr**ed, **pref**erence
    re**fer** → re**ferr**ed, re**ferr**ing, **ref**eree, re**ferr**al, **ref**erence

✓ Checkpoint B

First decide where the stress is and then add the suffixes given in brackets to these, doubling where necessary:
  1 omit (-ing) ....
  2 equip (-ed) ....
  3 target (-ing) ....
  4 benefit (-ing) ....
  5 regret (-able) ....
  6 ballot (-ed) ....
  7 budget (-ed) ....
  8 cosset (-ed) ....
  9 confer (-ence) ....
10 carpet (-ed) ....
11 transfer (-ing) ....
12 rivet (-ed) ....

7

TO DOUBLE ...?

Exceptions:

- words ending in 'l' (see below)
- worshipped   kidnapped   handicapped   formatted (and -ing endings for these)   transference   transferable

Note that the rule does not apply to words ending in:

- 'w', 'x' and 'y': renewed   outboxed   delayed
- two vowels and a consonant: repeated   repairing   maintained
- two consonants: rewarding   starting   warning

WORDS ENDING IN 'L'

If the word ends in 'l', double the 'l' when adding VOWEL-suffixes except -ity, -ise/-ize, -iser/-izer. It doesn't matter in this case where the stress is:

compel → compelling   cancel → cancelled   travel → traveller
propel → propelled

but with -ity and -ise: equality → equalise(r)   legality → legalise
More examples:

travel → travelled, travelling   quarrel → quarrelled, quarrelling
marvel → marvelled, marvellous   equal → equalled, equalling

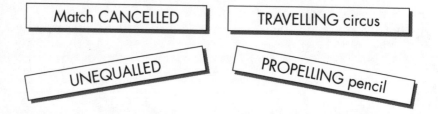

Exceptions: tranquil → tranquillity, tranquillise(r)
Note: don't double before consonant-suffixes: quarrelsome   instalment
fulfilment

✓ *Checkpoint C*

Add endings to the base words as indicated.

	base word	add suffix	word
	label	-ed	labelled
1	civil	-ise	....
2	travel	-er	....
3	enrol	-ment	....
4	equal	-ise	....
5	level	-ing	....
6	revel	-er	....

SUMMARY

When adding VOWEL-suffixes (like -ing, -ed)

1 Say the word aloud
2 Find the STRESS
3 If the stress is at the END or the word ends in 'l', DOUBLE
4 If the stress is NOT at the end, don't double
5 DON'T double when adding consonant-suffixes or when adding -ity or -ise(r) to words ending in 'l'.

Activities 1–7

1 Sort these words into groups, add **-ed** to each and write them in the correct column:

offer   permit   orbit   compel   travel   confer   fasten   annul   commit   prefer

doubled (stress at end)	not doubled (stress not at the end)	doubled (ends in 'l')
referred	murmured	cancelled
....	....	....
....	....	....
....	....	....
....	....	....

2 Fill in the gaps only where **necessary**.
   a   He fit_ed a new bathroom fit_ment.
   b   They equal_ed the record; he equal_ised with his goal.
   c   A din_er eats a din_er in a din_ing room.
   d   The fur_y beast was in a fur_y.
   e   The news sad_ened us; it filled us with sad_ness.
   f   She was refer_ing to his character refer_ence.
   g   I was non-commit_al, but he showed commit_ment.
   h   It was a strange occur_ence, and no one could say what had happen_ed.

3 Find the stress in these words and then add **-ing** to each. (Use a dictionary if necessary to check the stress.)
   Remember: Only double the last letter if the stress is at the **end** or the word **ends in 'l'**.
   a   docket ....
   b   picket ....
   c   differ ....
   d   packet ....
   e   deter ....
   f   benefit ....
   g   cosset ....
   h   cancel ....
   i   defer ....
   j   quarrel ....

4 Build up families of words, using the above rules and adding the suffixes given in brackets.

   a quarrel (-ing, -some) ....

   b prefer (-ed, -ing, -able, -ment) ....
    ....

   c refer (-ed, -ing, -ee, -al) ....

   d commit (-ed, -ing, -ee, -al, -ment) ....
    ....

   e market (-ed, -ing, -able) ....

   f cancel (-ed, -ing, -ation) ....

   g equal (-ed, -ise) ....

   h appeal (think about it!) (-ing, -ed) ....

   i allow (-ance, -ed) ....

   j orbit (-ed, -al) ....

5 Fill in the spaces.

PAYALOT is offe...ing, for a limi...ed period, low-price insurance. If you haven't already benefi...ed from our scheme or budge...ed for your retirement, write now for our quotation. Payments can be defe...ed (postponed).

No refe...ences required.

6 Fill in the gaps in this work report:

> John is commi…ed to his work and well-equi…ed mentally to
> succeed, though regre…ably he hasn't yet fulfi…ed his potential.
> However, he is now begi…ing to seize the opportunities offe…ed.

7 Fill in the blanks.
- **a** No trave…ers
- **b** Commi…ed person wanted
- **c** Remove wra…er
- **d** Begi…ing Monday
- **e** No cance…ations
- **f** Fishing permi…ed
- **g** Appa…ing tragedy
- **h** Account transfe…ed
- **i** Opportunities offe…ed

SKILLCHECK Check these statements to assess what you have
learned from this chapter. If you cannot honestly tick
all of these statements, then go back over the
relevant section of the chapter.

❑ I know when to double the final consonant before adding a vowel suffix.

❑ I know how to use the stress in a word to help with the spelling when
adding vowel-suffixes.

❑ I know what to do when adding consonant-suffixes.

8

ADVERBS

- **The -ly ending is usually the sign that a single word is an adverb. This is a word that tells you more about how, where, why or when something was or was not done.**
- **It describes a verb, or an adjective or another adverb.**

THE USUAL PATTERN

Do you know what happens when you add -ly to these words?
similar   cool   regular   careful   faithful   hopeful   final   actual
natural   basic   frantic   automatic   happy   crazy   temporary
simple   probable   incredible   true   whole   dull

> **RULE** The normal rule for making adverbs is **simply** to **add** -ly to the
> **base** word. Most words don't need any other change:
> quick + -ly → quickly   similar + -ly → similarly
> cool + -ly → coolly   extreme + -ly → extremely
> complete + -ly → completely   careful + -ly → carefully
> hopeful + -ly → hopefully   actual + -ly → actually
> final + -ly → finally

PARTICULARLY important   MORALLY wrong   CRUELLY treated
UNDOUBTEDLY true   CAREFULLY arranged

Be careful if the base word ends in a **silent** 'e'. Don't lose the 'e' – just add
-ly as normal:
rare + -ly → rarely   sincere + -ly → sincerely
immediate + -ly → immediately

DEFINITELY not	EXTREMELY dangerous
Yours SINCERELY	Ring IMMEDIATELY

Also: merely   accurately   desperately   approximately   intimately

If the base word ends in **-ful**, simply add -ly as normal:
careful + -ly → carefully   beauti + -ful → beautifully

And it's the same with words ending in **-al**, just add -ly:

    real + -ly → really   mechanical + -ly → mechanically

    equal + -ly → equally   general + -ly → generally

Yours FAITHFULLY

Drive CAREFULLY

SUCCESSFULLY completed

SPECIALLY baked

Is it REALLY?

CRITICALLY ill

PERSONALLY designed

Also: incidentally   eventually   physically   accidentally   technically

✓ Checkpoint A

Add **-ly** to these:
1 actual ....
2 peculiar ....
3 regular ....
4 truthful ....
5 skilful ....
6 occasional ....
7 logical ....
8 separate ....
9 sentimental ....
10 pitiful ....

EXCEPTIONS TO THE RULE

• Remember 'ic' needs an ally, so for words ending in **-ic** add **-ally** (not just -ly):

    basic → basic**ally**   drastic → drastic**ally**

(Originally the base word ended in '-ical' as in identical and critical, or in the old words tragical and fantastical.)

  It may help if you overstress the -ally when you say the word.

  Here are some more examples:

    frantic → frantically

AUTOMATICALLY re-wound   SPECIFICALLY geared to

    SCIENTIFICALLY speaking   FANTASTICALLY good looking

Also: terrifically   tragically   pathetically   spasmodically

There is only one exception: publicly

Add adverb endings to these:
  1 romantic ....
  2 diplomatic ....
  3 horrific ....
  4 apologetic ....
  5 enthusiastic ....
  6 moronic ....
  7 ironic ....
  8 characteristic ....
  9 sympathetic ....
10 realistic ....

- Words ending in a consonant + 'y' change the 'y' to 'i' before -ly:
    happy → happily   busy → busily   steady → steadily   tidy → tidily

    TEMPORARILY out of order   WITTILY put   Ding dong MERRILY
    It ain't NECESSARILY so   VOLUNTARILY manned

Also: crazily   daintily   heavily   primarily
Exceptions: shyly   wryly

- Words ending in a **sounded** 'e', like ample, humble, valuable, probable,
  drop the 'e' before -ly:
    amply   humbly   valuably   probably
    Here are some more examples:
    simple → simply   capable → capably   able → ably
    legible → legibly   subtle → subtly   responsible → responsibly

    PROBABLY the best   SUBTLY spicy   INCREDIBLY tasty
    UNBELIEVABLY good

Also: honourably   unforgivably

✓ *Checkpoint C*

Make adverbs from these:
1 unnecessary ....
2 pretty ....
3 sleepy ....
4 hasty ....
5 gloomy ....
6 lazy ....
7 extraordinary ....
8 sloppy ....

Make adverbs from these:
1 suitable ....   4 horrible ....
2 feeble ....   5 probable ....
3 terrible ....   6 noticeable ....

• Note that the one-syllable words true, due and whole become truly, duly and wholly. Full and dull become fully and dully:

> Yours TRULY   FULLY staffed   WHOLLY manufactured

SUMMARY

For most adverbs, simply add **-ly** (including words ending in a silent 'e', -ful and -al)

Exceptions: words ending in -ic, -y, -ble and -ple and some one-syllable words, like true, due and whole.

Activities 1–7

1 Complete these common adverbial expressions:
  a slow ...... but sure ......
  b real ...... and tru ......
  c Yours faithful ......
  d Yours sincere ......

2 Numerous words end in 'ology'. When they become adverbs, 'ology' becomes 'ologically'.
  Turn these words into adverbs:
  a geology ....   e physiology ....
  b technology ....   f meteorology ....
  c psychology ....   h biology ....
  d pathology ....

3 How many more words can you find ending in -ic and -ical? Add these to the examples below and then turn them into adverbs.

Words ending in -ic	Words ending in -ical
basic → basically	musical → musically

4 Change the words in brackets into adverbs ending in **-ly**, for example quick → quickly.

> Please ring John (immediate)_____. He's (accident)_____
>
> been held up.
>
> He's (probable)_____ OK and I'm (unnecessary)_____
>
> worried about him. (Basic)_____, though, I'd like
>
> to know (definite)_____.
>
> (Incidental)_____, I enjoyed the show (terrific)_____.
>
> Thanks,
>
>   B.

5 Make adverbs from the words in brackets and put them in the blank spaces.
(Undoubted) .... Joanna's speech was (subtle) .... and (witty) .... delivered. I (particular) .... liked her (extreme) .... clever jokes which went down so (successful) .... with the audience.

6 Triple adverbs. Make adverbs from the words in brackets.
  a I usually sign off with the words (true) .... , (faithful) .... or (sincere) ....
  b You have worked (careful) .... , (methodical) .... and (successful) ....
  c He raged (frantic) .... , (crazy) .... and (tragic) ....
  d She loved him (romantic) .... , (desperate) .... and (complete) ....
  e It functioned (natural) .... , (automatic) .... and (accurate) ....
  f We played (cool) .... , (serene) .... and (graceful) ....
  g You shouldn't overuse words like (terrific) .... , (fantastic) .... and (incredible) ....
  h They sang (simple) .... , (beautiful) .... and (unforgettable) ....

7 Fill in the appropriate adverb, formed from the word in brackets.

Adverbially speaking ...

Nothing had been (satisfactory) .... explained and no one was (particular) .... pleased to be summoned to a (hasty) .... arranged meeting in the drawing room.

'Sorry to bring you all here,' said Inspector Force (apologetic) ....

'This is (unspeakable) .... irritating,' said Lady Ponsonby (haughty) ....

'And I am (definite) .... not amused,' added Aunt Agatha (lofty) ....

'It's all so (complete) .... mystifying,' murmured Mr Mumbles (dreamy) ....

'(Extreme) .... ,' agreed Major Minor (simple) ....

'And all so (unnecessary) .... complicated,' moaned Mrs Simpleton (pathetic) ....

'I suppose we'll be here (positive) .... ages,' remarked Earl Gallbladder (gloomy) ....

'I shall (undoubted) .... leave when I choose,' announced Lord Chizzleham (obstinate) ....

'The whole thing is becoming (unbearable) .... boring,' muttered Bertie (weary) ....

SKILLCHECK Check these statements to assess what you have learned from this chapter. If you cannot honestly tick all of these statements, then go back over the relevant section of the chapter.

- ❏ I know how to add -ly to form an adverb.
- ❏ I know how to form adverbs from adjectives ending in -ful or -al.
- ❏ I know how to form adverbs from adjectives ending in -ic.
- ❏ I know how to form adverbs from adjectives ending in a consonant and 'y'.
- ❏ I know how to form adverbs from adjectives ending in -le where the 'e' is sounded.

9
CHOOSING THE
RIGHT ENDING

- You will need to know what a noun, an adjective and a verb are for this chapter.
- A **noun** names things, people, places or qualities, for example, doctor, vehicle, monastery, elegance.
- An **adjective** tells you more about a noun (or pronoun), for example, **identical** twins, **changeable** weather, a **terrific** thunderstorm.
- A verb expresses what is being done (or a state of being), for example, He **recognised** her, to **legalise**.
- It will also help you in this chapter to think of related words in instances where their spelling is clearer, for example, **luxurious, luxury**.

-ICAL, -ICLE, -ACLE

- **-ical** is a common **adjectival** ending:
   identical   technical   medical opinion

   PHYSICAL education   TECHNICAL college

- **-icle** and **-acle** are **noun** endings.
  You should be able to hear the difference if you say them slowly:
   vehicle   particle   icicle   article   tentacle   spectacle (spectacular)
   miracle (miraculous)   obstacle

-ER, -OR, -AR, -RE

These are mostly noun endings referring to a doer or an agent.

- **-er** often indicates an Old English word and an early or basic occupation:
   baker   maker   gardener
  but note: character   further   propeller   protester

- **-or** indicates a more modern activity or profession:
  solicitor   surveyor   professor   supervisor   sponsor   vendor
  author   governor
  Also conqueror   emperor

  VISITORS THIS WAY   DOCTOR'S SURGERY

  If you have trouble remembering these, try overstressing the ending.
- **-ar** as a noun ending is fairly rare. Learn the common ones:
  grammar (grammatical)   scholar (scholastic)   burglar (burglary)
  calendar   cellar   caterpillar
  CALENDAR month
As an adjective ending -ar is quite common:
  similar (similarity)   familiar (familiarity)   peculiar (peculiarity)
  particular
  SIMILAR situation   a PARTICULAR point
- **-re** Most words ending in a consonant followed by -re are nouns:
  calibre   fibre   metre

✓ *Checkpoint A*

1 Add **-icle**, **-ical** or **-acle** to these:
  a obst ......
  b pract ......
  c vert ......
  d cub ......
  e surg ......
  f cler ......
  g crit ......

2 Add **-er**, **-or** or **-ar** to these:
  a charact ......
  b solicit ......
  c calculat ......

-ARY, -ORY, -ERY, -URY

-ary and -ory **tend** to be adjective endings.
-ery and -ury are noun endings.

- **-ary** (adjectives): imaginary (imagination)   voluntary (voluntarily)
  primary   secondary   stationary (standing still)   hereditary

  PRIMARY SCHOOL   VOLUNTARY redundancies

(nouns): library (librarian)   granary   dictionary

LIBRARY: Quiet, please   English DICTIONARY

- **-ory** (adjectives): compulsory   supervisory
(nouns – these describe a place): laboratory   lavatory   dormitory

Greenwich OBSERVATORY

- **-ery** (nouns): monastery   stationery (envelopes, etc)

Highgate CEMETERY

- **-ury** (nouns): luxury (luxurious)   penury

Twentieth CENTURY

A few words end in **-try**: ministry   dentistry   artistry   carpentry

9

✓ *Checkpoint B*

Put the right ending (**-ary**, **-ory**, **-ery**, **-ury**) on these:
1 fact ......
2 centen......
3 invent......
4 veterin......
5 estu......
6 refect......

-TION, -SION, -SSION, -CIAN

All these endings denote nouns.
The **-ion** ending means a state of being.
The **-cian** ending indicates a person skilled in something.

- **-tion**: At least six out of every ten -ion nouns have the **-tion** ending which is usually pronounced 'shun'.
    If there is a verb in the word's family which ends in 't' or 'te' or 'fy', then the ending will normally be **-tion**: educate → education
satisfy → satisfaction

- **-sion**: Verbs ending in 'd' or 'de' lose their d/de and form nouns ending in -sion:
    persuade → persuasion   collide → collision   pretend → pretension
    comprehend → comprehension

Needs no PERSUASION

CHOOSING ENDINGS

- **-ssion**: The double 's' occurs when the base word or root ends in a double 's':

    possess → possession   express → expression   confess → confession

    Vacant POSSESSION   Honest CONFESSION

    Verbs with the root 'mit' (for example, permit, commit, admit) form nouns with -ssion:

    permit → permission   admit → admission   commit → commission

    No ADMISSION   No COMMISSION

    Verbs containing the root 'ceed'/'cede' (go) end in -ssion:

    proceed → procession   concede → concession

    No CONCESSIONS

- **-cian**: This indicates a person skilled at something:

    musician   mathematician   technician   physician   politician

✓ Checkpoint C

Form nouns ending in **-ion** from these:
1 prevent ....
2 pretend ....
3 omit ....
4 apprehend ....
5 profess ....
6 persuade ....

-OUS, -EOUS, -IOUS

These endings all mean 'full of' or 'like'.

- **-ous** occurs after a **complete** word that ends in a consonant:
  mountain → mountainous   danger → dangerous   marvel → marvellous
  If the base word ends in a silent 'e', drop this before -ous:
  ridicule → ridiculous
  Nouns ending in 'f' change to 'v': grief → grievous
  mischief → mischievous
- **-eous** The 'e' keeps the 'g' soft (like a 'j') in courageous   gorgeous
  outrageous
  Also learn these (you can hear the 'e'): simultaneous   miscellaneous
  spontaneous
- **-ious** The 'i' keeps the 'c' soft in spacious   gracious   delicious
  conscious, and keeps the 'g' soft in religious   sacrilegious

9

CHOOSING ENDINGS

Words ending in 'y' change to 'i': fury → furious   envy → envious
vary → various   mystery → mysterious
(See Chapter 6 for endings in **-or**ous like humorous, vigorous, glamorous.)

✓ *Checkpoint D*

Put the **-ous** ending on these. Make any other necessary changes.

1 melod ....
2 advantag ....
3 fam ....
4 relig ....
5 glor ....
6 feroc ....
7 griev ....
8 hid ....
9 prev ....
10 self-right ....

-ENT, -ANT (-ENCE, -ANCE, -ENSE)

Unfortunately, there are few guidelines for these, though -ent and -ence are more common.

- After a hard 'c' or 'g' (as in cat and goat), the **-ant** and **-ance** endings occur: elegant → elegance   significant → significance
- After a soft 'c' or 'g' (as in ceiling and giant) the **-ent** and **-ence** endings occur: negligent → negligence   magnificent → magnificence

FRAGRANT

ELEGANT

IMPORTANT

- **-ent** is the **adjective** ending in independent, dependent (upon) and confident (of)
- **-ant** is the **noun**: a dependant (but independ**ence**), a confidant

Here are some common words to learn. Invent a memory aid for the most troublesome:

CHOOSING ENDINGS   9

- **-ant, -ance**: RELEVANT relevance descendant PERSEVERANCE MAINTENANCE pleasant fragrant
- **-ent, -ence**: EXCELLENT excellence EXPERIENCE SENTENCE EXISTENCE DIFFERENT DIFFERENCE OCCURRENCE persistent persistence superintendent competent DEFENCE turbulence
- **-ense** EXPENSE suspense immense

✓ *Checkpoint E*

1 Add **-ent** or **-ant**:
  a eloqu....
  b promin....
  c excell....
  d ineleg....
  e relev....

2 Add **-ence** or **-ance**:
  a consequ....
  b confer....
  c persever....
  d persist....
  e sent....

-ABLE, -IBLE (-ABLY, -IBLY, -ABILITY, -IBILITY)

- **-able** is more common when adding to a **complete** word: returnable changeable commendable honourable favourable
  Learn these: probable available

  Tickets AVAILABLE Delays PROBABLE

  Where there is a verb in the word's family ending in **-a**te (or a noun ending in **-a**tion) the **-a**ble ending will occur: demonstrate, demonstration → demonstrable irritate, irritation → irritable
  Remember to keep the 'e' after the 'c' and 'g' (to keep them 'soft') in peac**e**able servic**e**able notic**e**able manag**e**able

- **-ible** tends to be added after incomplete words or roots: legible, responsible
  -ible is common after 's': visible feasible permissible

  Delays POSSIBLE VISIBILITY poor

  -ible occurs when there is a noun ending in -ion but **not -a**tion in its family: audition → audible combustion → combustible

✓ *Checkpoint F*

Put **-ible** or **-able** on these:
1 horr ....
2 indigest ....
3 irresist ....
4 uncontroll ....
5 prob ....
6 respons ....
7 notic ....
8 comprehens ....
9 elig ....
10 incred ....
11 unforgett ....
12 indestruct ....

-ISE, -IZE

• The **-ise** ending is usually acceptable. Some people like to keep the -ize ending (from the Greek 'izo') for verbs that mean making or altering something, for example, legalize, equalize, fertilize (or legalise, equalise, fertilise) but you can't use -ize for SURPRISE, supervise, devise, advise. -ise is therefore the 'safe' ending.
But note: analyse   paralyse

Activities 1–4

1 Fill in the blanks.
   What the critics say
   Excell......t   Outrag......, fast and fur......us (from fury) fun   A mir......c...... (marvel) of gorg...... spect....... (show)   A must for your calen.......r
2 Fill in the gaps.
   Charact......rs in play by imagin......ry auth......r
   Emper......r and conquer......r, Napoleon Bonaparte
   Volunt...... blood don......r and charity spons......r, Joe Public
   Profess......r and doct......r, Albert Einstein
   Local politi......n, solicit......r and school govern......r, C. Fox
   Garden......r and landscape survey......r, C. Brown
   Begg......r, living in monast...... cell......r
   Burgl......r
   Veh...... (car) mainten......ce supervi......r
   Mrs Miscellan......, working in local libr......y
   A mischiev......s caterpill......r
   Lavat......y attend......nt
   Groundsman in cemet......y

Laborat......y techni......n
Veterin......y surgeon
(Play spons......red by I. Winnapenny)

3 Fill in the missing letters in this jingle:
A diction_ _y's indispens_ ble.
It makes words comprehens_ ble.
You soon become famil_ _r
With spellings like simil_ r and peculi_ r.
Spelling has obvious relev_ nce.
It's a form of technic_ _ compet_ nce.
Like gramm_ r, it helps write a sent_ nce,
But you'll need to show persist_ nce.

4 In these exchanges Bob is extremely hard of hearing. Fill in the blanks.
ANNE   I hear you've got a veh...... (car) ident...... (like) to mine?
BOB   Ah yes, but the technic...... (scientific) term for an octopus's leg is a
      tent.......
ANNE   Have you calculated the expen......e (cost) of mainten......nce work?
BOB   Yes, Ecuador certainly has an imm......n......e (huge) amount of
      mountain......s scen......ry.
ANNE   Is this plan feas......ble?
BOB   Well, it's not vis......ble from where I'm standing.
ANNE   Are these napkins dispos......ble?
BOB   But no one's indispens......ble, sir.
ANNE   I gather he's been leading a very relig......s exist......nce?
BOB   I disagree and I think your last sent......nce is quite ridicul......s.

9

SKILLCHECK   Check these statements to assess what you have
learned from this chapter. If you cannot honestly tick
all of these statements, then go back over the
relevant section of the chapter.

❑ I know when to use -ical, -icle or -acle.

❑ I know when to use -er, -or, -ar or -re.

❑ I know when to use -ary, -ery, -ory or -ury.

❑ I know when to use -tion, -sion, -ssion, or -cian.

❑ I know when to use -ous, -ious or -eous.

❑ I know when to use -ent and -ence or -ant and -ance.

❑ I know when to use -able, -ably and -ability or -ible, -ibly and -ibility.

❑ I know when to use -ise or -ize.

10
PLURALS

- **Singular means only one, for example, a boy.**
- **Plural means more than one, for example, boys.**
- **A noun is a word that names a thing or a quality, for example, a person, a table, or beauty.**

Noun plurals are **usually** formed by simply adding **s** to the singular:
boy (singular) → boys (plural)
This includes words ending in 'e' like cake: cakes   valuables   catastrophes   recipes   similes
But, if the noun ends in an 's' type of sound, as in 's', 'ss', 'ch', 'sh', 'x' or 'z', you add **-es**: bus → buses   class → classes   glass → glasses
business → businesses   church → churches   bench → benches
sandwich → sandwiches   stitch → stitches   thrush → thrushes
bush → bushes   fox → foxes   fez → fezes (but quiz → quizzes)
In all these words you should be able to hear the 'e'.

Warning: Remember **not** to put an apostrophe in simple noun plurals where there is no idea of ownership:
The greengrocer sells apples, pears, plums, tomatoes, carrots, cabbages and potatoes.
None of these plurals needs an apostrophe. (See also Chapter 12.)
The apostrophe can only be used as a plural for **non**-words like letters and figures, for example, three A's, two 8's. Even here, it might be considered unnecessary.

Turn these into plurals:
1 box ......
2 princess ......
3 recipe ......
4 survivor ......
5 metaphor ......
6 pitch ......
7 witch ......
8 business ......

WORDS ENDING IN 'Y'

- If the word ends with a consonant + 'y' change the 'y' to 'ie' before adding 's': lady → ladies   baby → babies   lorry → lorries

✓ *Checkpoint B*

Turn these into plurals:
1 supply ....
2 lolly ....
3 enquiry ....
4 family ....

- If there is an 'e' (or any other vowel) before the 'y', just add 's': valley → valleys   chimney → chimneys   monkey → monkeys Wednesday → Wednesdays

✓ *Checkpoint C*

Turn these into plurals:

1 donkey	8 estuary ....
2 volley	9 jockey ....
3 trolley	10 century ....
4 diary	11 library ....
5 convoy	12 university ....
6 factory	13 facility ....
7 pulley	14 holiday ....

WORDS ENDING IN 'O'

- Most just add 's', especially if they are fairly modern or musical/Italian words: video → videos   biro → biros   piano → pianos   photo → photos   soprano → sopranos
- Some common words end in -es:
    TOMATOES   POTATOES

Also   heroes   cargoes   echoes   vetoes   mottoes   volcanoes   mosquitoes   embargoes   tornadoes
(For several words both -os and -oes are correct.)
    Use your dictionary when in doubt.

WORDS ENDING IN 'F' OR 'FE'

- 'F' at the end of a word often becomes -ves in the plural:
    loaf → loaves   half → halves   thief → thieves   leaf → leaves   wife → wives   knife → knives   sheaf → sheaves   calf → calves   wolf → wolves

You should be able to hear the 'v' when you pronounce these to yourself.

- For chief and roof (and proof, reproof) just add 's': chiefs   roofs
  Say them carefully.
- A few words can have either ending: hoofs or hooves   scarfs or scarves   handkerchiefs or handkerchieves   wharfs or wharves   turfs or turves.

OTHER GROUPS

■ FOREIGN WORDS

Some of these keep their foreign plurals, especially those words from Greek ending in -sis or -on (like criterion):
    crisis → crises   oasis → oases   phenomenon → phenomena   criterion → criteria
A few Latin ones: larva → larvae   cactus → cacti   stimulus → stimuli
Check with a dictionary when you need to.

■ HYPHENATED WORDS

These usually add 's' to the main part (or noun part) of the word:
    son-in-law → sons-in-law   passer-by → passers-by
but words like sit-in, lay-off or send-up (where an adverb – in, off, up – is attached to the verb), take the 's' at the end: lay-off → lay-offs
send-off → send-offs   lay-by → lay-bys   sit-in → sit-ins

■ NO CHANGE

A few words are the same in the singular and plural: sheep   aircraft   series

■ OLD ENGLISH PLURALS

A few words have Old English plurals like: child → children   man → men
woman → women   foot → feet

Activities 1–6

1 Put the plural form in the space provided. (The singular form is in brackets.)
Shopping list

a set of kitchen (knife) ....   1kg (tomato) ....
a book of vegetarian (recipe) ....   6 (biro) ....
2 lemon and 2 orange (jelly) ....   3kg (potato) ....
some Danish (pastry) ....   3 (loaf) .... of bread
2 (box) .... of wine (glass) ....   6 fruit (lolly) ....

Remember **not** to put an apostrophe in ordinary noun plurals.

2 Add the correct plural ending. (The singular is in brackets.)

a We looked at several (property) propert...... .
b Supermarket (trolley) troll...... .
c Happy (family) famil...... .
d (Journey) Journ...... to foreign (country) countr...... .
e No (reply) repl...... .
f Down the (valley) vall...... .
g The three (witch) witch............ and their (prophecy) prophec...... .
h Smoking (chimney) chimn...... on (factory) factor...... .
i He scored three (try) tr...... and two (penalty) penalt...... .
j (Hero) Her...... and (heroine) heroin...... .
k (Apology) Apolog...... received.

3 Remind yourself of the rules given above.

a Give the plural form of the following and group them under the correct heading:

rally   echo   roof   alley   cemetery   chimney   gigolo   ally   sundry
potato   valley   thief   library   sandwich   take-off

plurals in -ies	plurals in -eys	other
ladies	jockeys	benches
....	....	....
....	....	....
....	....	....
....	....	....
....	....	....
....	....	....
....	....	....

4 Write out the number as a word and turn the noun in the brackets into the plural in the following:

a 14 .... (giraffe) ....

b 40 .... (monkey) ....

c 8 .... (bush baby) ....

d 18 .... (pony) ....

e 80 .... (donkey) ....

f 90 .... (calf) ....

5 Put the bracketed words into the plural in these advertisements:

a

PLANTS AND TREES FOR SALE

(ivy) ...., (cactus) ....,

Michaelmas (daisy) ....,

ornamental (grass) ....,

day (lily) ...., (iris) ....,

(narcissus) ...., (gladiolus) ....,

(cypress) ...., silver (birch) ....

TO CLEAR –
ex-service stock

army (lorry) ....,

car (battery) ....,

metal (shelf) ....,

inflatable (dinghy) ....,

(jersey) .... from

foreign (army) ....

and (navy) ....

WANTED two (secretary) .... to work for compilers of (dictionary) ....; experience of working in (university) .... desirable; excellent (facility) ....;
ring 012345 for (enquiry) ....

6 Put the bracketed words into the plural.
Early explorers were not only (hero) .... but also (survivor) .... of various (crisis) .... and (catastrophe) ...., including deadly (mosquito) ...., poisonous (gas) .... and erupting (volcano) ....

SKILLCHECK Check these statements to assess what you have learned from this chapter. If you cannot honestly tick all of these statements, then go back over the relevant section of the chapter.

❏ I know how to form the plural of words ending in 'y'.

❏ I know how to form the plural of words ending in 'o'.

❏ I know how to form the plural of words ending in 'f' and 'fe'.

❏ I know how to form the plural of hyphenated words.

❏ I know how to form the plural of common groups of foreign words.

11
A SUMMARY OF ENDINGS

BRIEF CHECKLIST FOR MAIN RULES

1 Silent 'e' at end of base word (See Chapter 6.)

- This normally drops when adding a **vowel**-suffix   *excite → exciting*
- but not when adding a **consonant**-suffix   *excitement*

Exception: *argument*

2 To double or not to double? (See Chapter 7.)

- Double the end of the base word for words of **one** vowel ending in a consonant   *tap → tapped   tapping*
- For longer words ending in **one** vowel and **one** consonant, for example, ad**mit** and or**bit**:
  a double if the stress is at the **end**   *ad**mit**ted*
  b don't double if it's not   *or**bit**ed*

3 'y' to 'i' (See Chapter 6.)

- 'y' changes to 'i' before all suffixes except **-ing**
  happy → happiness   marry → married but *marrying*
- But **not** if there's a vowel before the 'y'   *journey → journeyed*

4 Adverbs (ending in -ly) (See Chapter 8.)

- Normally just add **-ly**   *immediate → immediately*
  Watch out for words ending -al and -ful which also add -ly
  dismal → dismally   careful → carefully
- For words ending in -ic, add **-ally**   *basic → basically*
- For words ending in -ple and -ble, drop the 'e' and add -ly
  simple → simply   probable → probably

5 Plurals (See Chapter 10.)

- Normally just add 's' *boy → boys*
- But add 'es' if the word ends in an 's' type of sound (s, sh, ch, ss, x, z) *church → churches* *glass → glasses*
- If the word ends in a consonant + 'y' change to 'ie' + 's' *lady → ladies*
- If the word ends in a vowel + 'y' just add 's' *valley → valleys*

(Note: Don't put apostrophes in simple noun plurals where there is no idea of ownership.)

TRICKY ENDINGS

-able, -ible (See Chapter 9.)

- Normally just add to the base word or root *return → returnable*
- Drop the silent 'e' *response → responsible*
- Keep the silent 'e' after 'c' or 'g' to keep them 'soft' *notice → noticeable* *manage → manageable*

-ant, -ance (See Chapter 9.)

-aid

- *say → said* *pay → paid* *lay → laid*

-al

- Only one 'l' *occasional* *accidental*

-ally (See Chapter 8.)

- Note double 'l' *real + ly → really*

-ically (See Chapter 8,)

- Add -ally to words ending in -ic *basic → basically*

-ar, -er, -or (See Chapter 9.)

-ary, -ery, -ory, -ury (See Chapter 8.)

-ce, -se (See Chapter 5.)

- The noun has a 'c' *a practice*
- The verb has an 's' *to practise*

-es (See Chapters 8 and 10.)

- After words ending in 's' sounds like bench and gas, add -es *benches* *gases*
- Do the same for verb forms *he pushes* *she passes* (see -ies below.)

-ed (See Chapters 6 and 7.)

- Normally, just add to the base word   return → returned
- Drop the silent 'e'   care + ed → cared
- Double the last letter of words with one vowel + consonant
  tap → tapped
- In longer words double if the stress is at the end   com**mit** → committed
- Don't double if the stress is **not** at the end   **or**bit → orbited
- Double if the base word ends in 'l'   travel → travelled
- Change 'y' to 'i' in words ending in a consonant + y   marry → married
- Insert 'k' after 'c'   picnic → picnicked
- For words ending in 'w', 'x', 'y', don't double   followed   decoyed
- For words ending in two vowels and a consonant, don't double   repeated
- For words ending in two consonants, don't double   warned   farmed

-eys (See Chapter 10)

- For words ending in -ey just add 's'
  donkey → donkeys   journey → journeys

-ful

- This always ends in one 'l'

-fully (See Chapter 8.)

- This always has two 'l's   careful → carefully

-ing (See Chapters 6 and 7.)

- Normally just add to base word   return → returning
- Drop the silent 'e'   care → caring
- Double the last letter of one-syllable words ending in one vowel + one
  consonant   tap → tapping
- In longer words ending in one vowel + one consonant, double if the stress
  is at the end   re**fer** → referring
- Don't double if the stress is **not** at the end   **of**fer → offering
- Double if word ends in 'l'   travel → travelling
- Keep the 'y'   marry → marrying   carry → carrying
- Keep the 'e' in canoeing   singeing (burning)   dyeing (colours)
- Put a 'k' after the 'c'   panic → panicking

-ies (See Chapter 10.)

- If word ends in consonant + 'y' change to **-ies**
  lady → ladies   marry→marries

A SUMMARY OF ENDINGS

-ical, -icle, -acle (Chapter 9.)

-ically (See Chapter 8.)

- words ending in -ic form adverbs with **-ically**   *basic → basically*

-ing (See Chapter 6.)

-ise/ize (See Chapter 9.)

- It's safe to use -ise
- Don't double the 'l'   *legalise*

-ity (See Chapter 12.)

- Don't double the 'l'   *equal → equality*

Exception: *tranquillity*

-ion

- (For -tion, -sion, -ssion, -cian see Chapter 15.)

-hood, -less, -ment, -ness (See Chapter 11.)

- Consonant-suffixes are normally just added to the base word
  manhood   excitement   keenness   hopeless

Exception: *argument*

- But 'y' changes to 'i'   *lively → livelihood   merry → merriment*

-ly (See Chapter 8.)

- Just add -ly for most adverbs   *sincere → sincerely   extreme → extremely*
- This includes base words ending in -al and -ful
  really   carefully   accidentally
- But add -ally to base words ending in -ic   *basic → basically*
- Change 'y' to 'i'   *happy → happily*
- Note: *true → truly   due → duly   whole → wholly*

-ous (For -orous see Chapter 6 and for -ous, -ious and -eous see Chapters 6 and 9.)

-s (See Chapter 10.)

- For plurals normally just add 's'   *boy → boys*
- But see -es, -eys and -ies above.
- Don't put an apostrophe in a normal noun plural where there is no idea of ownership.

11

A SUMMARY OF ENDINGS

1 Add **-ing** to these. Write out the complete word.
 a mimic ....
 b prefer ....
 c notice ....
 d omit ....
 e argue ....
 f tie ....
 g fly ....
 h appeal ....
 i hoe ....
 j appal ....
 k survey ....
 l panic ....

2 Match the word listed below to the category. Ask yourself what each base word is.
Category 1: longer words ending in one vowel + one consonant with the stress at the end.
Category 2: longer words ending in one vowel + 'l'.
Category 3: words of one syllable with one vowel + one consonant at the end.
Category 4: longer words ending in one vowel + one consonant with the stress not at the end.
Category 5: words ending in consonant + 'y'.
Category 6: words ending in a double vowel + one consonant.
Category 7: words ending in one vowel + 'y'.
Category 8: words ending in a vowel + consonant + silent 'e'.

word	category	word	category
occurring	....	modelling	....
delayed	....	applying	....
swimming	....	staring	....
committed	....	budgeted	....
dining	....	travelling	....
preferred	....	beginning	....
offering	....	devising	....
propelled	....	riveting	....
benefited	....	repeated	....
shinned	....	carrying	....

11

A SUMMARY OF ENDINGS

3 Fill in the blanks in these job advertisements:

Sales Representative

Required immediat......
Applic......ts should have
relev......t and successfu ......
market......g experi......nce,
preferab......y recent. Sal......ry
depend......nt on experi......nce.
Letter of application should be
accompan......d by the names and
addres...... of two refer......s.

HOUSING MANAGER

The successfu...... applic......nt
will be respons......ble for liaison
with the statut......ry agenc......s
in both the volunt......ry and
public sect......rs. He/she will be
expected to plan programm......s
strategic......y and work on
commit......es. Business and
secreta......l skills would be
advantag......us. Travel......ng
expen......es p......d.

The Volunt......ry Cen...... for the Handica......ed requires a healthcare worker

Applic......nt should be famil......r with
and commit......d to working with the
physic......y handica......ed.

Prefer......ce given to applic......nts
technic......y profic......nt in the field of
physiotherapy. Driv......ng licen......e
particul......y valu......ble. Excell......nt
facilit......s avail......ble. Initia......y
offer......d as a tempor......ry post but
could be perman......nt.

4 Fill in the blanks in these notes for film reviews:

a

The Shield of Arthur

Typic......y extravag......nt adventure in which legend......ry her......s eas......ly
overcome dangers. Magic......y evoked atmosphere. Scenic......y beautifu......, but
charact......rs very forget......ble.

b

ARROWS OF DESIRE

Critic......y acclaimed and phenomen......ly successfu...... film
about physic......y handica......ed boy's quest for Olympic Gold.
Direct......r Wills fulfil......ng all the promise of his earlier
films. Compe......ing (from compel) perform......nces.

c

RIVER OF BLOOD

Exception......y vic......us and horrific......y repell......nt film about
mass-murder......r. Outrag......us scenes of gratuitous viol......nce.

d

Porkies

Irresist......bly humo......ous film about glamo......ous heroine's
fantas......s for gorg......usly fat men. Subt......y and wit......ly
played. Definit......y not to be missed.

12
PUNCTUATION
AND
SPELLING

- **'CREAM TEA'S and HOT MEAL'S.'** Did you spot the mistakes?

Many people would find this difficult.

- **'Alot of people can not understand this, infact.'** How many mistakes are there in this sentence? You should have spotted three – the correct versions are a lot of, cannot and in fact.
- A football manager once wrote in a club programme:
  'I hope all my good players will resign next season.'
  He meant re-sign. A hyphen, as you can see, can be important.
- And someone who writes a letter applying for a job saying he or she is taking 'english in june' isn't likely to impress.

THE APOSTROPHE

■ USING THE APOSTROPHE TO SHOW OWNERSHIP

The idea of possession or belonging is shown by adding an apostrophe and an 's' to the 'owning' noun, for example, that lady's hat (the hat belonging to that lady) or a week's holiday (a holiday **of** a week). This does not apply to words like mine, yours, ours and theirs, because these are not nouns but pronouns, which do not take an apostrophe.

- In the singular (just one) the apostrophe comes **before** the 's':
  that lady's hat (one lady)
- In the plural (more than one) the apostrophe goes **after** the 's':
  those ladies' hats (the hats of those ladies)

Be careful, however, with plurals that do **not** end in 's':
  men   women   children
  In these cases the apostrophe comes **before** the 's':
  men's shoes   women's rights   children's toys

Note: **don't** put the apostrophe in ordinary noun plurals where there is no idea of ownership.

> The greengrocer sells apple**s**, pear**s**, plum**s** and tomato**es** (all without apostrophes).

And **don't** put the apostrophe in ITS when the meaning is BELONGING TO IT.

The only time an apostrophe is sometimes used for simple plurals is with non-words like figures and letters, for example, three 8's, four A's. Even here, you don't really need them. It's (meaning it is) best to keep the apostrophe for where IT'S really needed.

▪ USING THE APOSTROPHE TO SHOW WHERE LETTERS HAVE BEEN LEFT OUT

Where two words are shortened into one, and one or more letter is dropped, the apostrophe is put in place of the missing letter(s): *I'm* is short for *I am*

Be specially careful of these:

- it's (short for *it is* or *it has*): It's raining.   It's finished now.
- doesn't (short for *does not*): It doesn't work.
- can't (short for *cannot*)
- we're (short for *we are*)

EVERYTHING'S IN ITS PROPER PLACE, I'M PLEASED TO SAY.

STORE GUIDE

Children's clothes	2
Children's toys	G
Ladies' shoes	2
Ladies' clothes	1
Men's clothes	B
Men's shoes	B

- you're (short for *you are*) and aren't (short for *are not*): You're sure about this, aren't you?
- they're (short for *they are*): They're off!
- there's (short for *there is* or *there has*): There's been another false start. There's nothing they can do about it.

Also: won't (short for *will not*, originally shortened from Middle English 'wol not') shan't (short for *shall not*. This used to be shortened as sha'n't.)

Note: the only way you can shorten *must have, would have, could have* and *should have* is *must've, would've,* and so on. **Never** use 'of'.

✓ *Checkpoint A*

1 Turn these into the possessive form using an apostrophe, for example, 'the pen belonging to the boy' becomes 'the boy's pen':
   a the hair of the girl ....
   b the hair of the girls ....
   c the cargo of the ship ....
   d the cargoes of the ships ....
   e the efforts of the English team ....
   f the toys belonging to the children ....
   g a holiday of three weeks ....
   h the crying of the babies ....
   i the work of a whole month ....
   j the tails of the mice ....

2 Put the words in brackets into the shortened form using the apostrophe, for example, 'did not' becomes 'didn't'.
   a (There is) .... no doubt about it. (We are) .... done for.
   b You (will not) .... know (it has) .... happened.
   c (I would) .... be careful if I were you.
   d (It is) .... a common mistake.
   e It looks odd, (does it not?) ....
   f (You are) .... very welcome.

ONE WORD OR MORE?

- Each of these is just **one** word:
   although   cannot   tomorrow   straightforward (simple)   alright (OK)
   whereas   upstairs   downstairs

   I CANNOT come TOMORROW.

12

- These are **two** or **more** words:
  in fact   in front   in between   in spite of   as well   a lot of   lots of
  no one

  A LOT OF lovely lolly   'AS WELL' is two words IN FACT.

- Sometimes (now and then)   **but**   some times are better than others
  When it is two words it has the sense of single or particular times.
  (See also Chapter 1 for words like 'already' and 'all ready'.)

HYPHENS

Hyphens are used when joining two or more words to make another word:
    short-term   poverty-stricken
Often hyphenated words drop the hyphen and become single words:
    multi-storey → multistorey   multi-coloured → multicoloured.

It's best to keep the hyphen

- to avoid confusion, as with resign and re-sign, recover and re-cover,
  (recover health but re-cover upholstery), reform and re-form (form again)
- for words made up of more than two other words:
  a couldn't-care-less attitude
- when the prefix (the part added to the beginning) is followed by a proper
  name (the name of a particular person, place or thing):
  mid-Atlantic   late-Victorian

CAPITAL LETTERS

These are used:

- to begin sentences: They said they were leaving.
- for the first word in a speech: They said, '**We**'re leaving now.'
- for names of **particular** people, places, things (proper nouns)
- for days of the week and months of the year
- for adjectives (words that describe nouns) derived from proper nouns:
  English   Victorian
- for the pronoun **I**
- for initials: BBC   ITV   UNESCO
- for God and anything of His or to do with Him
- when something is seen as a person (for example, Father Time, Mother
  Earth) or an abstract quality is personified.

✓ Checkpoint B

Read the following postcard and notice all the times when a capital letter is used. Make a list of the words with a capital letter and give a reason each time.

Dear Jane and Simon,
It's Wednesday the 10th of August, and my second day in Spain. We flew to Marbella yesterday (with BA) and have an apartment near Paradise Beach. There are lots of English people here, but also Spanish, German and Dutch. The sun is out, so it's out with the Umber Solero and I'm feeling ready for summer romance. (I'm reading 'Love on the Shore' to get me in the mood!) All it needs is for a tall, dark, handsome stranger to say, 'Do you come here often?' The answer, sadly, is 'No', but I'm going to enjoy it while it lasts. See you in a fortnight.

Mandy.

✓ Checkpoint C

Write out the following, putting the correct spacing between words. Put in all necessary capitals, apostrophes and hyphens.
1 infrontofthefrenchgreengrocersshoptherewerenoticesinenglishadvertising coxsorangepippinswilliampearsandsevilleoranges.
2 itsnothisorhersbuttheirs.
3 ashesjustoutofhospitalhecannotgoupstairsordownstairsstraightawaybut tomorrowhemaybeableto.

Activities 1–4

1 What is the difference between
  a fifty-odd people and fifty odd people
  b a number of big-vehicle owners and a number of big vehicle-owners
  c They were all most helpful and they were almost helpful.
  d That expensive umbrella needs to be re-covered and recovered.
  e MAN EATING SHARK and MAN-EATING SHARK?

2 Proofread this, putting the correct choice in the blanks:

Buy 'DOGGO'

(Dogtired/Dog-tired) .... with the boring old brands of dog food?

(Noone's/No one's) .... told you about 'DOGGO'?

It (dosent/doesn't) .... matter if (there/their/they're) .... (retrievers/retriever's) .... or dachsunds, (yorkshire/Yorkshire) .... terriers or (Irish/irish) .... setters, they'll all love (their/there/they're) .... 'DOGGO'. (It's/its) .... the best thing since (butcher's/butchers/ butchers') .... bones.

So don't be a (doginthemanger/dog-in-the-manger) ...., the sort who (let's/lets) .... your pet put you in the doghouse. Buy 'DOGGO' (tomorrow/to morrow) .... (Let's/lets) .... let every dog have (its/it's) .... day, and especially (yours/your's) .... See it cavorting (infront/in front) .... of the neighbours.

See it cheerfully chasing cats (in between/inbetween) .... the cabbages.

(Alotof/a lotof/a lot of) .... happy dog-owners everywhere buy their pets 'DOGGO'. Why not buy (yours/your's) .... some (as well/aswell) .... and give new meaning to the phrase '(Its/it's) .... a (dogs/dog's/dogs') .... life?

(May be/maybe) .... dogs (can not/cannot) .... speak (english/English) ...., but they'll definitely bark for 'DOGGO'.

3 Mainly capitals: list all the words that should begin with a capital letter in the following notes for an introductory letter to a pen friend.

i'm joan... studying english and business studies at bradchaster college. my birthday is 4 june (under sign of gemini). my favourite day of the week's friday. my ideal place for my holiday is the caribbean or mediterranean.
sometimes i read the independent, sometimes the guardian. the tv programme i never miss is coronation street. i prefer scotsmen to welshmen (there's a story behind that). i hate christmas. i love victorian dolls.

4 Proofread this:

INTERVIEWER Judy, if a boy asks you out, say for to morrow night, and you
             dont want to go, whats your reply?

JUDY   I say i've got too much work to do and cant possibly make it, all
             though infact im probably doing nothing.

INTERVIEWER And if he insists inspite of that?

JUDY   Well, if he dosent get the message I tell him my works very
             important or that ive got an appointment or some other date, or
             i'm going to wash my hair – i've got alot of excuses. . . .

INTERVIEWER But what do you say if you want to accept?

JUDY   Yes, ofcourse.

INTERVIEWER And if you want to ask a boy out, whats your approach?

JUDY   I just ring him up and tell him i've nothing to do and that theres a
             good film on at the cinema.

INTERVIEWER And if he dosent respond?

JUDY   I ask him for the next day aswell or suggest we could meet any
             time.

INTERVIEWER So you dont give up.

JUDY   No, I wont take no for an answer!

SKILLCHECK   Check these statements to assess what you have
                  learned from this chapter. If you cannot honestly tick
                  all of these statements, then go back over the
                  relevant section of the chapter.

❑ I know when to use an apostrophe.

❑ I know when *not* to use an apostrophe.

❑ I know how to use hyphens.

❑ I know when to spell a word with a capital letter.

12

13

2 5 0 K E Y
W O R D S

- There are about 250 words that account for over 70 per cent of all spelling errors.
- It makes sense, then, to work hard at these, preferably a few at a time.
- Use the learning methods and tips given in the Introduction.
- The first of the two lists below has been arranged according to the main chapters of this book. The second list is alphabetical for speedy checking.

LIST A: THE MOST COMMONLY MISSPELT WORDS GROUPED BY RULES

1 COMMON WORDS
- *across   among   until   paid   laid   view   forty   scene   ninth   speech   doesn't*
- *quarter   tying (knots)   fourteen   forest   finish   building   minute   family   agreeable   bargain   argument   thorough   necessary*

2 WORDS OFTEN CONFUSED (Chapter 1)
it's (it is, it has), its (belonging to it)   their (belonging to them), there (in that place, there is/are), they're (they are)   who's (who is/has), whose (belonging to whom)   passed (the verb – he passed), past (all other uses)   lose (mislay, fail to win), loose (untied)   to affect (alter), effect (result)   a practice (noun), to practise (verb)   to accept (receive), except (not including)   principal (chief), principle (law, rule)

3 PRONUNCIATION RULES (Chapter 2)
- ie/ei If sound is 'ee', then 'ie' except after 'c'
  a *believe   achieve   mischievous*
  b *deceit   receive   conceited   receipt*
If the sound is not 'ee', then 'ei'   *height   foreign   neighbours   leisure*

Exceptions *friend   seize   weird*

drop 'e' before -ing: *exciting   arguing   coming*

4 PRONUNCIATION DIFFERENCES (Chapter 3)
*business   secretary   interested   description   decision   descend
undoubtedly   vegetable   pursue   medicine   twelfth   February
primitive   parliament   arctic   murmuring   conspiracy   temporary
temperature   intellectual   involved*

5 WORD-FAMILIES AND ROOTS (Chapter 5)
- French   *surprise   maintenance   manoeuvre*
- Latin   para (set) *preparation, separate*   sci (know) *conscious,
  conscientious*   fini(end) *definite*   rid(laugh) *ridiculous*   cog (know)
  recognise   hibit (hold)   *exhibit*
- Companion words: *prejudice (judicial)   privilege (legal)
  consensus (sense)   concentrate (centre)*
- Greek   *character   rhythm   atmosphere   technique   hypocrisy*

6 PREFIXES (Chapter 5)
- Just add   *disappoint   disappear   address   unnecessary
  interrupt   withhold*
- Adapt   *accommodation   acquaintance   acquire   aggression
  appear   different   occasion   occurrence   opposition
  opportunity   successful*   (Note: *proceed   procedure*)
- one 'l'   *welfare   fulfil*

7 ADDING CONSONANT-SUFFIXES AND SOME CHANGES WHEN
ADDING VOWEL SUFFIXES (Chapter 6)
- Just add consonant-suffix   *careful   excitement   grateful
  meanness   drunkenness   development   advertisement
  government   environment*   But *awful   skilful*
- 'y' to 'i'   *try → tries   marriage   loneliness   likelihood*
  Keep 'e' or 'i' for soft 'c'/'g':   *noticeable   manageable
  knowledgeable   courageous   religious   vicious*
- Insert 'k' after 'c' before -ing, -ed, -er   *picnicking   panicked*
- -our to -orous   *humorous*

8 TO DOUBLE OR NOT TO DOUBLE? (Chapter 7)
- Stress at end   *beginning   committed   committee   permitted
  referring   preferred   occurred   unforgettable*
- Stress not at end   *offered   happened   developed   benefited
  fastening*

13

Exception *worshipped*

- Double the 'l' *traveller   quarrelling   fulfilled   appalling marvellous   woollen*
  also *tranquillity*

9 ADVERBS (Chapter 8)

- Just add -ly *extremely   sincerely   immediately   particularly completely   merely   desperately   similarly   gradually   skilfully really   incidentally   accidentally   occasionally   physically beautifully   carefully*
- -ic to -ically *basically   drastically   terrifically*

Exception *publicly*

- drop 'e' *probably   subtly   truly   duly   wholly*

10 PLURALS (Chapter 10) and *One word or more?* (Chapter 12)

- Plurals: *tomatoes   potatoes   valleys   chimneys   centuries*
- One word or more? *in front (2)   in fact (2) in spite of (3)   a lot of (3)   as well (2)   no one (2)   tomorrow (1)*

11 WHICH ENDING? (Chapter 9)

- -ent/-ence *sentence   existence   experience   persistence permanent   excellent   independent*
- -ant/-ance *elegant   relevant   extravagant   perseverance*
  Note: *expense*
- -or, -ar *visitor   professor   solicitor   burglar   grammar calendar*
- -ary, -ery *library   cemetery*
- -icle, -acle *vehicle   miracle   article*
- *politician*

12 A MIXED BAG
favourite   defence   possession   detached   parallel   tyranny tragedy   criticism   attach   embarrass   exercise   exhilarating honourable   disastrous   balance   comparison   adequate recommend   exaggerate   ecstasy   lightning (flash)

LIST B: THE MOST COMMONLY MISSPELT WORDS LISTED ALPHABETICALLY

accept (*receive*)
accidentally
accommodation
achieve
across
acquaintance
acquire
address
adequate
advertisement
affect (to influence)
aggression
agreeable
a lot of (3)
among
appalling
appear
arctic
arguing
argument
article
as well
atmosphere
attach
awful

balance
bargain
basically
beautifully
beginning
believe
benefited
building
burglar
business

calendar
careful
carefully
cemetery
centuries
character
chimneys

coming
committed
committee
comparison
completely
conceited
concentrate
conscientious
conscious
consensus
conspiracy
courageous
criticism

deceit
decision
defence
definite
descend
description
desperately
detached
developed
development
different
disappear
disappoint
disastrous
doesn't
drastically
drunkenness
duly

ecstasy
effect (*result*)
elegant
embarrass
environment
exaggerate
excellent
except (*not including*)
excitement
exciting
exercise

exhibit
exhilarating
existence
expense
experience
extravagant
extremely

family
fastening
favourite
February
finish
foreign
forest
forty
fourteen
friend
fulfil
fulfilled

government
gradually
grammar
grateful

happened
height
honourable
humorous
hypocrisy

immediately
incidentally
independent
in fact (2)
in front (2)
in spite of (3)
intellectual
interested
interrupt
involved
its (*belonging to it*)
it's (*it is, it has*)

13

knowledgeable

laid
leisure
library
lightning (*flash*)
likelihood
loneliness
loose (*untied*)
lose (*fail to win/mislay*)

maintenance
manageable
manoeuvre
marriage
marvellous
meanness
medicine
merely
minute
miracle
mischievous
murmuring

necessary
neighbours
ninth
no one (2)
noticeable

occasion
occasionally
occurred
occurrence
offered
opportunity
opposition

paid
panicked
parallel
parliament
particularly
passed (*verb*)
past (*other uses*)
permanent
permitted

perseverance
persistence
physically
picnicking
politician
possession
potatoes
practice (*noun*)
practise (*verb*)
preferred
prejudice
preparation
primitive
principal (*chief*)
principle (*law*)
privilege
probably
procedure
proceed
professor
publicly
pursue

quarrelling
quarter

really
receive
receipt
recognise
recommend
referring
relevant
religious
rhythm
ridiculous

scene
secretary
seize
sentence
separate
similarly
sincerely
skilful
skilfully
solicitor

speech
subtly
successful(ly)
surprise

technique
temperature
temporary
terrifically
their (*belonging to them*)
there (*in that place,* and
 in *there is, there are*)
they're (*they are*)
thorough
tomatoes
tomorrow
tragedy
tranquillity
traveller
tries
truly
twelfth
tying (*a knot*)
tyranny

undoubtedly
unforgettable
unnecessary
until

valleys
vegetable
vehicle
vicious
view
visitor

weird
welfare
wholly
who's (*who is, who has*)
whose (*belonging to
 whom*)
withhold
woollen
worshipped

1 Fill in the gaps.

You're am......ng fr......nds. Good wages p......d. Keep your bal......nce on the tightrope. Stop im...d......t......ly (straightaway). Finest v......ws in the county. Fantastic barg......ns. Open unti...... September. Caution ne......s......ry (needed): b......lding site. Trekking a......ross Africa. He'll be com......ng in a qua......t...... (¼) of an hour. Give the house a tho......gh cleaning. My fav......ite singer. Her stirring sp......ch drew loud applause.

2 Proofread:

CAP-IT-ALL
THE WONDERWASH

- **Eggsiting new devvelloppment in washing technology**
- **Conserntrated capsule with micro-active afect**
- **Reely stubborn stains dissapere imeedyatly**
- **Leaves wulens byootifuly finnished**
- **Garanteyed fiber-frendly and enviromentaly safe**
- **A quatre of the price of ordinary powders**
- **Reckomended by all washing-machine manufacturers**

250 KEY WORDS

13

3 Fill in the blanks.

Beat the Beasties

Desp......rate about those spelling demons?

Are you embar......sed by your dis...str......us and ap......l......ng errors?

Break the spell. Break l......se (free) from the tyr......ny of the 250 Key Words. S......ze the op......rtunity. Suc......ss g......ranteed.

You, too, could be a skil......u...... (full of skill) speller with this revolutionary new tec......ni...... (method). Even the most vi......ous (nasty) vil......ns (criminals), like 'r......t......m' (the beat in music) or 'ac......m......dation', will succu...... (surrender) to your spellbinding power.

4 Fill in the spaces.

The Person......l Manager 10 Feb......ry 1995
Blank Pharmaceuticals
Blankton

Dear Sir,

Chemic...... Develop......ent Techni......n

I am writing in response to your adverti......ment in last Tuesday's edition of The Independ......nt Chemist.

I am e......n (18) years old and am int......ested in a career in which I can develo...... my knowle......e and int......est in s......entific subjects, partic......ly Chemistry and Physics. I pas...... both subjects at GCSE, ach......ving a grade B in each. I also pas...... in English Lang......ge, Math......atics and Comput......r Studies.

I would espec......ly we......ome the op......rtunity to a......uire (obtain) furth......r qualifications such as those refe......ed to in your advertis...ent.

I have some previous experi......nce of lab......r......ry work, having done a hol......day job while at school. This ......nvolved setting up ap......ratus, carr......ing out chemic...... prep......rations and monit......ring reactions.

My curr......nt job in the Pla......ing Depart......ent of the Borough Coun......l is ch......fly cleric...... and does not offer the scope that I would like to develo...... in a technic...... f......ld.

I should be glad to supply any furth......r information you consider ne......s......ry (needed).

You......s faithfu......y,

Rachel Wilson

5 Fill in the gaps.

Sp......ch to Coun......l Meeting

I was delighted to rec......ve your letter inviting me to sp......k on behalf of the Hambridge Conservation Society. I am most gr......ful (thankful) for the op......tunity to ad......ess the Coun......l on the subject of the proposed hypermarket.

Am......ng local inhabitants it has been s......d (past of say) that th...... are many dif......r......nt and op......sing v......ws (opinions). A tho......gh (full) survey of our members reveals that three-qu......s (¾) support the argu......ent that a hypermarket should not be all......d (permitted) to cut into Knightly Oak For......st, an area of outstanding nat......al beauty.

The advantages offe......ed by the sc......me (plan) have, we bel......ve, been exa......rated (overstated). Any rel......f from traffic congestion will be offset by the loss to local b......s......ess (trade). Many of us feel, too, that the village has already p......d too dearly for recent pla......ing d......sions.

We therefore urge you to refuse permi......ion for this develop......ent, which we bel......ve will have a dev......stating ......fect on the enviro......ent.

14

FURTHER ACTIVITIES

1 Fill in the gaps.

a CAR BOOT ITEMS FOR SALE

wool......s (made of wool), sand......s (soft shoes), wom......'s (ladies') handkerch......s, me......'s (for men) pyj......mas, s......s......rs (to cut with), furn......ture

b Barbe......ue he...... (in this place) tom......w (next day) We......day, w......ther permi......ng

c Contributions gr......fu......y rec......ved

d T......sday's Television Programmes Channel 10:

Tom......r......w in Parl......ment; N......ghbours, Fr......nds and Famil......s; Funny Fav......rites; Defen......e after the N......clear Deter......nt; Op......rtunity Knocks; A......ross the Ar......ic (near North Pole) with the Eskim......s; A V......w (look) of the Urban Enviro......ent; Car...... b......an (West Indian) Calypso.

e *Shopping list*

> *potat......s, tomat......s, a fresh veg......able, let......ce,*
> *sau......ages, something to barbe......e, bisc......ts,*
> *des......c......ted (dried) coc......nut, marg......rine,*
> *mayo......se (salad cream), cig......tes*

2 *Scrabble*

Add prefixes and suffixes to the base word or root on the board, using the letters on the tray. (Revise Chapters 5, 6 and 7 if necessary.)

.... CIDENT	Tray: LCALYAE	Answer: ACCIDENTALLY
a .... FORGET	Tray: LYAUTBN	Use all 7 letters.
b .... DOUBT	Tray: YDNLEUP	Use 6 letters.
c .... APPEAR	Tray: SAINDEC	Use all 7 letters.
d .... NATURAL	Tray: DOYNIUL	Use 4 letters.
e .... RULE	Tray: ROEDNTV	Use 5 letters.
f .... SCIENTIFIC	Tray: AYLNCLU	Use 6 letters.
g .... APPOINT	Tray: TSEIDNM	Use all 7 letters.

3 Correct this letter.

Dear Sir
   We aknollege the reciet of your order of the twelfth of febuary. The goods will be despached (carridge payed) by freyt from our supplyer. Assureing you of our imedeate attention at all times,

   Your's faithfuly

   Paul E. Spelt

4 Fill in the blanks.

PEPINO'S PESTO

The tr......ly Italian taste, su......t......e (delicate) flavour and ir......sist......ble fragr......nce of Pepino's Pesto is internation......ly ren......ed (famous). Made from whol......y nat......ral ingredi......s to a specia......y formulated rec......p...... and vac......m-packed in our own lab......r......t......s. Enjoy it with your fav......rite pasta. Keep in the refr......erat......r.

5 Fill in the spaces.
Guest's Garage
Veh......e maint......n......ce carr......d out by prof......s......nal mec......nics to the highest specifications. D......sel engines a special......ty.
Customer's instructions: Adjust ac......l......r......t......r p......d...... (foot control); fill up with ant......-freeze; repair transmi......on system; test alternat......r; remove tail-pipe of ex......st and replace; mend pun......red t......re; beat out body pan......ling.

6 Complete the crossword.

CLUES
ACROSS: 4 aroused **6** completed or very satisfied **8** disaster **11** presented or provided **12** by chance
DOWN: 1 apart, differently, not done together **2** place, especially in a play **3** it's none of your . . . . **5** without a doubt **6** more than just an acquaintance **7** widespread; also army chief **9** near the North Pole **10** fail to win or to find

7 Fill in the blanks:

Careers Guidance from:

Ath......tics Coach, Army Col......el, Assist......nt Com......sioner of
P......l......ce, Auth......r, Chartered Survey......r, Coll......ge Princip......,
Doct......r of Med......cine, F......ld Mar......al, For......n Attaché, Garage
Mec......nic, Gard......er, Gover......ent Inspect......r, Lab......r......t......y
Tec......i......n, Libr......ian, Local Counc......l......r, L......tenant (RN),
Magazine Edit......r, Mar......ge Coun......l......r, Math......mati......n,
Met......r......logist, Minister for the Envir......ent, Mor......age Arranger
(arranges a loan for a house), N......c......r Ph......c......ist,
Pers......n......l Officer, P......l......ce Superintend......nt, Politi......an
(for example, Member of Parl......ment), Pr......st (any religion),
Prof......s......r of Lit......ature, Ps......c......trist (for mental problems),
Ps......c......logist (studies human behaviour), Relig......us
Kno......le......e Teacher, Ser......nt Major, Shep......rd, Sol......er (in the
army), Sol......c......t......r's sec......t......ry, Spe......ch Therapist

8 Fill in the gaps in this curriculum vitae (cv).

Name: ....
Ad.........ress: .... Age: ......

Experi......nce:

1993–1995: Ac......m......d......tion Officer, respons......ble
for li......son (links) with housing trusts

1990–1993: Sec......t......ry to Pers......n......l Officer,
Wilco

1987–1990: Sec......tarial Assist......nt in local
gover......ent (pla......ing depar......ent)

Education:

1986–1987: Keynote's Secr......tarial Colle......e

1983–1986: Topton Terti......ry Colle......e

1977–1983: Tanglewood Tec......nic...... Colle......e

Int......ests and Activities

Com......t......ee member of local l......sure (recreational)
cent......, ...nvolved in swim......ng instruction and
maint......n......ce of sports facilit......s

FURTHER ACTIVITIES

14

9 Complete these.
Estate agent's advertisements

a

Val......b......e (worth having) op......rt......ty to a......uire (obtain)
prestig......us b......s......ness premi......es of......ring
ex......e......l......nt ac......m......dation. Also lux......ry
ap......rt......ents for prof......sionals with n......ghbouring l......sure
(for rest and play) facilit......s.

b

First advertis......ent: Partic......l......y spac......us (full of space)
tha......hed (roof made of reeds) c......r......cter cot......ge with
b......tifu...... (lovely) v......ws.

c

At......active semi-deta......hed maison......te with at......ched garage,
sep......r......te di......ing room (for eating in); manag......ble garden.

10 *Scrabble*
Add prefixes and/or suffixes to the word or root on the board, using the
letters on the tray. (Revise Chapters 5, 6 and 7 if necessary.)
.... CEPTION ....   Tray: YLXELNA   Use 6 letters
Answer: **EXCEPTIONALLY**

a	.... NECESSAR	Tray: LNILUYN	Use 5 letters.
b	.... CASION	Tray: YCLAOLE	Use 6 letters.
c	.... ADVANTAG	Tray: SIEDUOS	Use all 7 letters.
d	.... COMPAN	Tray: MTCEANI	Use all 7 letters.
e	.... CHARACTERISTIC	Tray: LNKULYA	Use 6 letters.
f	.... GRESS	Tray: VYGEAIL	Use all 7 letters.
g	.... NOTIC	Tray: ENALUEB	Use all 7 letters.
h	.... CONTROL	Tray: BNALLUE	Use all 7 letters.
i	.... REGRET	Tray: ALTOBYN	Use 5 letters.
j	.... CANCEL	Tray: TNLSOIA	Use all 7 letters.
k	.... RESPONS	Tray: BRLIIYS	Use 6 letters.
l	.... CESSF	Tray: YSUULCL	Use all 7 letters.

11 Fill in the gaps.
a Notes for *A Travel......'s Guide to Ecuador*:
Adjacent to Colombia and Peru – has var......ty of climate and
enviro......ent, from equator......l for......st and Andean plat...... (high
flat land) – capit......l Quito – n......ghbouring volcan......s
ap......oximat......y 6000 met......s in h......ght – to tropic......
vall......s – Guayaquil on an est......ry has 'pea-soup' atmos......re and
temp......tures of 80 Fa......enheit – relativ......y stable gover......ent –
ef......c......nt (works well) transport system for trave......ing around –
Galapagos I......ands, 'lab......rt......y of evolution' – rec......m......ded
to the visit......r for tru......y phenom......nal wildlife in bar......n
(desert) scen......ry.

b *Travel Agent's advertisement*

> Bo......d (fed up) with Brit......n? You could be hol......daying in the
> Car......b......an, golfing in the Portug......se Algarve or sun......ng yourself
> on the Med......t......r......nean i......and of Cyp......s. Or you could be
> travel......ng in Hung......y and the C......ech Republic or even enjoying an
> ex......ting (full of adventure) Ar......tic (near North Pole) experi......nce.

12 Wordsearch:

There are fifteen separate words for you to find. All of them are horizontal or vertical and contain common roots.

T	P	E	C	X	E	B	J	N	D	W	F	V	N
V	A	X	M	Y	C	E	T	I	N	I	F	E	D
G	B	C	F	I	N	I	T	E	T	X	U	N	C
E	Q	I	P	R	E	O	G	W	P	H	P	T	O
H	C	T	R	U	I	Y	X	N	E	B	M	Y	N
L	D	E	E	L	C	L	R	G	C	L	I	G	S
M	I	B	P	D	S	U	O	I	C	S	N	O	C
O	S	N	A	Q	M	G	J	S	A	R	F	S	I
V	R	P	R	K	O	P	W	S	Q	E	I	T	E
S	U	T	A	R	A	P	P	A	D	N	N	V	N
N	P	L	T	I	B	I	H	X	E	X	I	A	C
N	T	U	O	J	G	U	X	P	V	M	T	L	E
E	T	A	R	A	P	E	S	D	Z	C	Y	B	T
D	E	I	Y	C	N	S	K	I	L	F	U	L	R

13 Complete this:

SATANIC RITES IN DEVON CEMET......RY

'Sacr...l......ge,' says local vic......r

The vic......r of Newton Bumbleford expressed shock at the w......rd (strange) practi......es rum......red (according to gossip) to have oc......red (taken place) in the local cemet......ry. N......ghbouring famil......s complained of strange happen......gs last Tuesday night. 'There se......ms to be evidence of people worship......ng prim......tive id......s (false gods),' he told reporters. 'If so, it's blas......my,' he added.
Members of other local relig......us com......nit......s (groups) condem......ed the acts as outrag......us.

REPORTS EXAG......RATED

A Devon Humanist Society spokesman commented: 'It's obviously some misch......v......us prank.' Local resid......ts reported alc......l (drinks) cans in their gardens.
The recent folk festival has at......acted (drawn to it) a convoy of travel......rs. 'They were singing hy......s (holy songs) and ps......ms,' sa......d (commented) local postmistress, Mrs Patt.
New-Age travel......rs claimed the reports were exag......rated. 'We're victims of pre......udice yet again,' they said. 'We were just hav......ng a rave.'

14 The following report has been 'forged'. Correct all the wrong spellings:

> *COLLEDGE REPORT on* I.M.A. Forger
>
> **Mathmatix:** A concienshus and comited skoler who's suckses's in arithmatik and statistix have been unparrallellled in my teeching experience.
>
> **english Litrature:** Ivan undoutably has the suttelty of mind and the criticle abbillity to martial rellevent works of refferrance aswell as to anerlize arguement.
> It has been a privyledge to teech him.
>
> **FIZZIX:** Ivan has truely remarquable powers of conserntration. He is pertickly efishent in his skillfull applyence of syentifik tekneeks and in useing labortry aperaytuss.
>
> ***************************
>
> Ivan is to be complemented on the exellance of his atcheevments both akademmicly and on the athelitix feeld.
> I am most greatfull two him for his valubul work on the collidge dissiplinery comitee.
>
> *A. Misspeller*, Collidge Principle

15 Complete the crossword.

CLUES

ACROSS: 1 memorably (adverb) **3** happened
6 main or principal **8** part of a play or a place **9** grab
10 opposite of presence **12** female of nephew **13** in a well informed way

DOWN: 1 not needed **2** taken or accepted **4** mentioning
5 straightaway **7** to trust (in) **8** ends with a full stop or a punishment **11** under a window

16 Fill in the spaces.

Victory for Tamchester United

Tamchester United s......zed their op......rtunity to clinch the prem......r leag...... title today with an ex......ting win over Portwich. In two ......nspired spells of dis......plined and dev......stating ag......ession, they routed the op...sition who are now condem......d to relegation.

After a qu......t opening qua......t...... of an hour, crowd-fav......rite Jackie Drake, making a wel......ome comeback to the side, dec......ved (tricked) the f......r (4)-man Portwich def......e and slot......d (put in the slot) the ball saf......y into the net. ...... (18) min......tes later, after some ski......fu...... passing, team-mate Jim Matthews, United's ch......f goalscorer, rec......ved a car......f......ly l......d-off pass from Drake to d......spa......h (send) a f......rcely struck shot pas...... goalie Green.

United, finding their true r......thm, added furth......r to their score when Tommy Shanks's ex......ting b......c......cle (bike) kick ricoch......ed off the post to dec......ve a bewildered keeper. Min......tes later, the Portwich defender, Jones, ap......r......ntly (seemingly) obliv......us (unaware) to the danger, was g......lty of an ap......ling (awful) back-pass which was gr......t......ly (thankfully) snap......d up by Deacon who scored with the most clinic...... of voll......s.

The tide of ag......ession now ir......sist......ble (not to be resisted), United were soon furth......r ahead, Drake scor......ng a marvel......us goal following some su...t......e (clever) footwork in front of goal.

The half-time whistle couldn't come soon enough for the rel......ved visit......rs who must have w......ndered what had hit them. The second half, however, brought temp......ry (for a short time) rel......f when Brooks, recently signed from Ugglepool, was rewarded for his persist......nce.

United, however, were not to be den......d furth......r goals, as, much to Portwich's embar......sment, Drake completed his hat-trick with a ski......f......ly flighted lob over the now desp......rate op......sition goalie.

Two more goals followed in rapid suc......sion, one from Banks in the ...... (80th) min......te and the other from Shanks whose display must have impressed the England coach might......ly.

Fin......ly, in front of an e......static crowd, Drake added his .... (4th) to give United their biggest victory of the season.

It augurs well for the European camp......n (battle) begi......ng (starting) in September. ●

17 *Spellbound* (a spelling game for two groups)
Divide the group into two teams with someone (for example, a teacher) as quizmaster and scorer. Each team member takes a word to spell chosen by the quizmaster from a particular chapter of this book (like The Key Words List). If he or she gets the spelling right he/she scores two points; if he or she gets it wrong, any member of that side may answer it correctly for one point. (It can then be offered to the opposing team for one point.)

Ask members of each side, alternately, until everyone has had a turn (or decide how many rounds to play in advance).

(You can include penalties for getting it wrong, like writing the word out five times!)

18 So you want to use ten-letter words rather than play safe with three letter ones? Complete the following:
The European Com......nity remains a contr......ver......l (argued over) contemp......ry (of this time) issue, and the lack of con......us (general agreement) am......ng politi......ns of both part......s is evidence of this.

Some Conservative MPs are even prepared to put the gover......ent's parl......ment......ry majority in j......pardy (risk), bel......ving that they are representing the v......ws (opinions) of their constit......ts (voters). They see recent develop......ents as pre......udicial (harmful) to national sover......nty and consider Brussels bur......r......cy (red tape) wasteful. Consequently they seek to nego......iate new terms for Brit......n.

Op......nents of these opinions em......asise (stress) the con......e......tration (coming together) of com......rcial (trade) markets offer......d by he Com......nity, this being v......wed (seen) as universa......y ben......f......cial. The EU's com......tment to the defen......e and maint......n......ce of employees' rights is regarded as invalu......ble while the target......ng of resources to regional need is also signific......nt.

19 Fill in the blanks.
Medical notes
D......scription of symptoms

Pat......nt A: F......rty-year-old pat......nt admit......d suffer......ng from hyp......thermia with abnorma......y low blood temp......ature. At risk from ......eumonia. Lab......r......t......y tests reveal serious prot......n defic......ncy. Pat......nt complains of stoma...... aches and diar......a.

Pat......nt B: E......ty (80)-year-old pat......nt suffer......ng from acute r......matism and as......ma (breathing problems). Hyp......sensitive to drugs. Has had ph......siotherapy.

Pat......nt C: E......h (8)-year-old pat......nt with catar...... and ......ma (skin disease). Previously in......culated against di......theria. Hyp......active. History of ......chiatric (mental) care.

ANSWERS

Self-assessment questionnaire (page 6)

1 a We don't know where we're going.
b Are their friends there, too?
c There's no doubt that it is past her bedtime.
d I wonder whose car that is and who's parked it like that.
e Is this your doing? Look what you're doing!
f It is far too hot to go to the cinema.
g A piece of slate must have fallen off the roof.
h The injury didn't seem to have any effect on her performance since she was still first past the winning post.
i Let's consider the principal reasons for going.
j They will all accept the invitation except John.
k The cat was quite quiet, hoping to lose the dog by lying low under the bushes.
l I hear that you were allowed to go to the party.

2 a (i) dining shining stunning panicking pursuing
(ii) courageous advantageous
(iii) noticeable manageable
(iv) picnicked wrapped pinned planned mimicked
b receive retrieve friendly neighbours ceiling achieve seize weight height conceited niece chief believe heirloom relieve perceive

3 Only five are correct:
a business interesting involved
b medicine mischievous burglar (correct)
c vegetable literature description
d twelfth century (correct) contemporary
e generally secretary recognise
f luxury temperature primitive
g fastening (correct) desperate environment

h athletics (correct) particularly peculiarly
i necessary February intellectual
j disintegrate library (correct) undoubtedly

4 a disappoint disappear dissimilar
b withhold interruption acknowledge
c proceed immediate opponent
d commotion forecourt acquire
e overrule aggression conscious
f definite illegible accommodation
g enormous ridiculous suppose
h welfare antidote skilful
i unnatural separate surprise
j descend acclaim immodest

5 a (i) drunkenness noticing stubbornness
(ii) manageable achievement marriage
(iii) vigorous arguing pursuing
(iv) caring government admiring
(v) excitement humorous sloping
b (i) hungrily loneliness surveying
(ii) tidiness likelihood supplying
(iii) copied weariness business
(iv) liveliness lying happiness
(v) giddiness shabbiness moodiness

6 a swimming beginning transferring
b submitting scaring omitting
c riveting orbiting profiting
d developing murmuring appalling
e benefiting happening quarrelling
f committing propelling galloping
g offering travelling pocketing
h occurring worshipping concealing
i regretting preferring forgetting
j referring permitting balloting

7 a exceptionally   fantastically
extraordinarily
b coolly   drastically   publicly
c incidentally   immediately
accidentally
d truly   sincerely   simply
e dramatically   probably
faithfully
f automatically   happily   wholly
g tragically   terrifically   humbly
h carefully   subtly   really
i unnecessarily   peculiarly
similarly
j frantically   extremely   normally
8 a cemetery   imaginary   century
relevant   independent   elegant
magnificent   excellent   visitor
familiar   governor   solicitor
peculiar   grammar   calendar
b responsible   agreeable
valuable   noticeable
changeable   collapsible
c marvellous   religious   luxurious
mischievous   outrageous
humorous   disastrous
advantageous   glamorous
9 a ladies   thieves   tomatoes
b benches   valleys   chiefs
c glasses   supplies   wives
d chimneys   shelves   surveys
e allies   volleys   businesses
f lay-bys   heroes   ponies
g potatoes   libraries   phenomena
h children   send-offs   crises
i spoonfuls   lorries   roofs
j factories   gases   witnesses
10 a tomorrow   upstairs
straightaway   whereas   as well
in fact   in spite of   short-term
American   doesn't   children's toys
b (i) Our local stationer's seems to
sell a lot of Christmas gifts
and children's games,
whereas yours doesn't.
(ii) In spite of all the English
team's efforts to recover their
lost form, no one managed to
score, although the team was
playing in front of a home
crowd.
(iii) The Women's Institute has, in
fact, already held its annual
meeting.

Words often confused
(page 10)
Checkpoint
1 a Whose is it? It's mine.
b Let's see. There you are then.
c But you're cheating. There's
nothing there. Where did you hide
it?
d I don't know. It must have slipped
through my fingers.
2 There is no doubt that their singing is
not what they're famous for.
3 He had already gone past me before
he passed me the ball.
4 This tooth is so loose that I'll probably
lose it.
5 If he lets us, then let's do it
6 There were too many for all of us to
have a game.
7 They agreed to accept all the entries
except mine.
8 Practice makes perfect, so make sure
you practise.
9 Yesterday he was lying in the bed
where he had lain for the past two
weeks, but today the nurses have laid
him on a sunbed outside.
10 His principal concern was for the
moral principle involved in the case.

Activities 1–6
1 a current   licence   check   tyres
brakes   ensure   stationary
affect   braking   dual
principal
b passed   led   quiet   role
principal   revues   plum   serial
2 a The perfect Christmas gift –
personalised stationery.
Is your business stationary? We'll
get you on the move!
b The only cereal with 60 per cent
fruit!
Don't miss Channel 4's exciting
new serial.
c Is it time to review your finances?
Talk to us!
For a hilarious night out – nothing
better than an evening of comic
revue.
d A brilliant piece of theatre with
stars in all the major roles.
It's no party without Mini-Savoury
rolls!

3 a Is this the party of high moral standards?
Morale among back-benchers at an all-time low

b Britain and Europe – how many miles apart?
Six Britons killed in aircrash over Japan

c Teenage idol dies of overdose
Minister calls homeless 'idle'

4 Sample letter:
Dear Bill,
It's (it is) good to **hear** that **you're** (you are) back in circulation, recovering from the op. and **its** (of it) after-**effects** (results).
Let's (let us) hope the injury won't **affect** (cause a change in) your game of darts.
See you **here** soon,
Fred.

5 a dose (of medicine etc.); doze (rhymes with hose) – snooze
disease (pronounced 'diz-eeze') – illness; decease (pronounced 'de-cease') – death
en**ve**lop (verb) – surround; **en**velope (pronounced **onv**-velope) – cover for a letter
differ (stress on **diff**-) be unlike; defer (stress on -**fer**) – postpone

Pronunciation as a help to spelling (page 18)
Checkpoint A
1 a mating
b sniping
c declining
d shaking
e admiring
f amusing
g writing
h interfering
i arguing
2 a cared
b arrived
c striped
d queued
3 a careful
b fateful
c disgraceful
d shameful

Checkpoint B
1 a snipping
b skinning
c robbing
d sitting
2 a patted
b rotted
c batted
d skimmed

Checkpoint C
1 a wrapper   wrapping
b recliner   reclining
c robber   robbing
d debater   debating
2 a winning
b whining
c wiping
d whipping
e pursuing
f hitting

Checkpoint D
1 a He bared his chest to the elements. The way was barred.
b The road sloped gently down the hill. He slopped water all over the table.
c She planned her essay carefully. The carpenter planed the piece of wood.
d His hair was all matted. The two pandas eventually mated.
e She was scared of spiders. The cut on the face scarred him for life.
f She stripped the pine table of its old varnish. He preferred the striped jumper.
g She pined away with grief. He pinned the card on the board.
2 a The boxers were sparring in the ring. They were sparing no expense.
b They all enjoyed the wining and dining. By dinning tactics into the team the coach helped them to start winning.
c The bosun was piping the captain aboard. He won the race by just pipping his rival at the post.

Checkpoint E
1 a fastening
b profiting
c occurring
d fidgeting
e conferring

2 a permitted
b prohibited
c deterred
d regretted
e targeted
f benefited

Checkpoint F
1 equalling   equalise
2 quarrelsome   quarrelling
3 realise   reality
4 labelled   labelling
5 marvelled   marvellous
6 totalling   totality
7 excellent   excelled

Checkpoint G
1 relief
2 sovereign
3 leisure
4 conceited
5 shield
6 weight
7 handkerchief
8 freight
9 grief

Checkpoint H
1 peaceable   serviceable
2 frolicking   mimicking
3 outrageous   advantageous

Activities 1–5
1 writing   hopping   running   having
planned   shopping   hoping
swimming   diving   saving
spotted   taking   fitting   snapped
dragging   hoping   improving
coming
2 a chief
b achieve
c deceive
d besiege
e reign
f believe
g sovereign
h neigh
i yield
3 a smoking   damaging
b picnicking   tarmacked
c thieves   series   vicious
d receive   written   guarantee
e guilty   trafficking   seize
foreigners

4 shrieking   arguing   opened
caring   wrappings   admiring
friends'   interfering   mischief
disguising   receiving
handkerchiefs   intriguing   fatiguing
5 'ee' sound but not after c: priest
relieve   believe
'ee' sound and after c: perceive
receive   deceitful
not the 'ee' sound: veil   leisure
exceptions: seize   species

Pronunciation and spelling – differences (page 28)
Checkpoint A
1 chocolate
2 surprise
3 arctic
4 twelfth
5 February
6 Wednesday
7 chestnut
8 fasten
9 subtle

Checkpoint B
1 solemnly   condemned   primitive
grievous
2 intellectual   luxury   library
3 mathematics   involves   arithmetic
statistics
4 gnarled   knotted   knuckles
5 particularly   interested   literature
century
6 generally   recognised   involves
perspiration   inspiration   certainly
inspires   admiration
7 police   description   burglar
fastenings
8 undoubtedly   mischievous   attempt
debts
9 chocolate   subtle   cocoa   coconut
vegetable
10 Parliament   environment
government   politicians   decisions
affect   their   constituencies
11 Wednesday   eighth   twelfth
February
12 arctic   temperatures   autumn
effect   vegetables

Activities 1–6
1 secretary   grateful   familiar

information technology eighteen
business experience interested
opportunity solicitor's addresses
sincerely

2 **a** fastening handkerchief
pre-packed sandwiches
aspirins chocolate vegetable
diamond receipts picture
family

b Arctic temperatures February
Meteorological information
mountain inhabited shepherds
generally climbers expeditions
exhausted eight separate
attempts

3 **a** burglar hundred umbrellas
jewellery (or jewelry)

b athletics eighth century

c intellectual disintegration

d equipment Arctic expedition

4 **a** perspiration inspiration eighth
definitely recognise (or
recognize) primitive exhausted
subtle rhythms deteriorated
ridiculous pantomime
desperate attempts involve

b building sand-castles pursued
anemones Ghost Island
action-packed exciting
surprises memorable
descriptions many-tentacled
undoubtedly interesting
literature

c probably satirist medicine
hypocrisy chauvinism parody
parliamentary privilege
old-fashioned

5 **a** mon-**a**st-**e**ry cem-**e**t-**e**ry
es-tu-**a**ry sim-il-**a**r-ly cat-**e**g-**o**ry
grad-u**a**l-ly dem-oc-r**a**cy
h**y**p-oc-r**i**sy

b det-**e**r-ior-ate psy-chol-**o**gy
it-in-**e**r-ary par-tic-u-l**a**r-ly
con-tem-p**o**r-ary un-nec-**ess-a**r-ily
ex-tra-ord-**in-a**r-ily

c pro-n**u**n-ci-a-tion
ad-van-tag**e**-ous tec-hn**iq-ue**s
em-b**a**rr-**ass**-m**e**nt

6 Sample list:
bough enough borough
through thought cough

Using a dictionary (page 34)

Checkpoint A

1 **co**sseted
2 **be**nefited
3 de**fer**red
4 **ri**veted
5 **plum**meted
6 pre**fer**red
7 com**mit**ted

Checkpoints B and C

Dictionary exercises

Activities 1–3

1 **a** courteous
  b charade
  c schizophrenic
  d pseudonym
  e cipher (or cypher)
  f chauvinism
  g charisma
  h taut
  i knowledge
  j psalm
  k aisle

2 Dictionary exercise

3 Dictionary exericise

Word families (page 41)

Checkpoint A

1 mis + laid
2 inter + rupt
3 ex + cite
4 with + hold
5 mis + shapen
6 dis + agree
7 dis + similar
8 sur + round
9 sur + prise
10 de + scribe
11 de + scend
12 ad + dress

Checkpoint B

1 accelerate
2 aggravate
3 appoint
4 approve
5 arrears
6 attend
7 approach

Checkpoint C
1 commend
2 commit
3 corrupt
4 immortal
5 irrelevant
6 irresponsible
7 occur
8 opposition
9 suffix
10 suppress
11 suppose

Activities 1–9
1 Some examples:
  a eloquent elocution loquacious interlocutor soliloquy
  b postpone transport impose suppose position exposition
  c avert inverted advertisement transverse perverse subversion
  d revoke irrevocably invoke provoke provocation vocal convocation
  e contradict dictate predict indictment diction
2 Some examples:
  a telephone phonetic symphony euphony
  b democracy bureaucracy meritocracy
  c chronology anachronism chronicle chronic
  d psychology psychiatric psychedelic
  e scenery scenic scene scenario
  f geography autobiography autograph telegraph photograph
3 Dictionary exercise
4 a admiration
  b grateful
  c definite
  d perspiration
  e memorable
  f author
  g expedition
5 a ante-natal
  b hypothermia
  c proceeding
  d proscribed
6 allocated acquire opposite forecast withheld

7 a illogical
  b irregular
  c irresponsible
  d immobile
  e unnatural
  f irreversible
  g ignoble
  h unnecessary
8 Wordsearch
  Across: commit refuse exert oppose suppose resigned
  Down: withhold relapse surprise corrupt except overrules
9 aggrieve collapse compress oppress suppress appoint acquit correct compose oppose suppose announce approximate accustom aggravate annihilate occur occasion

Adding endings to words
(page 50)
Checkpoint A
1 management
2 barrenness
3 eventful
4 clueless
5 advertisement
6 woeful
7 development
8 enticement

Checkpoint B
1 enjoys enjoyed enjoyment
2 surveys surveying surveyed
3 volleys volleyed volleying

Checkpoint C
1 satisfying satisfied
2 envying envied
3 replying replied
4 livelihood
5 appliance
6 emptiness

Checkpoint D
1 advantageous
2 changeable
3 gorgeous

Checkpoint E
1 panicking tying
2 adventurous rigorous disastrous vaporous
3 sparing occupying dyeing dying

Activities 1–3

1
  a paid
  b daily
  c picnicking
  d tried
  e curiosity
  f laid
  g arguing
  h dyeing
  i loneliness

2 noticeable improvement business said cheerily noticing replied gloomily replying applied supplied denying likelihood business easily paid arguing trying business lying occupying livelihood funnily said disagreeing

3 Mini-scrabble
across: untidily tries
down: funniest paid business tying

To double or not to double?
(page 57)

Checkpoint A

1 begging potting putting hugging
2 dropped skinned tripped sparred
3 sadder robber runner wetter
4 sadness wetness fitness
5 sadden hidden rotten

Checkpoint B

1 omitting
2 equipped
3 targeting
4 benefiting
5 regrettable
6 balloted
7 budgeted
8 cosseted
9 conference
10 carpeted
11 transferring
12 riveted

Checkpoint C

1 civilise
2 traveller
3 enrolment
4 equalise
5 levelling
6 reveller

Activities 1–7

1 Doubled (stress at the end):
permitted
conferred
committed
preferred
Not doubled (with stress not at the end):
offered
orbited
fastened
Double (ends in 'l'):
compelled
travelled
annulled

2
  a fitted fitment
  b equalled equalised
  c diner (eats a) dinner dining
  d furry (beast) fury
  e saddened sadness
  f referring reference
  g non-committal commitment
  h occurrence happened

3
  a docketing
  b picketing
  c differing
  d packeting
  e deterring
  f benefiting
  g cosseting
  h cancelling
  i deferring
  j quarrelling

4
  a quarrelling quarrelsome
  b preferred preferring preferable preferment
  c referred referring referee referral
  d committed committing committee committal commitment
  e marketed marketing marketable
  f cancelled cancelling cancellation
  g equalled equalise
  h appealing appealed
  i allowance allowed
  j orbited orbital

5 offering limited benefited budgeted deferred references

6 committed equipped regrettably fulfilled beginning offered

7 **a** travellers
   b committed
   c wrapper
   d beginning
   e cancellations
   f permitted
   g appalling
   h transferred
   i offered

Adverbs (page 64)

Checkpoint A
1 actually
2 peculiarly
3 regularly
4 truthfully
5 skilfully
6 occasionally
7 logically
8 separately
9 sentimentally
10 pitifully

Checkpoint B
1 romantically
2 diplomatically
3 horrifically
4 apologetically
5 enthusiastically
6 moronically
7 ironically
8 characteristically
9 sympathetically
10 realistically

Checkpoint C
1 unnecessarily
2 prettily
3 sleepily
4 hastily
5 gloomily
6 lazily
7 extraordinarily
8 sloppily

Checkpoint D
1 suitably
2 feebly
3 terribly
4 horribly
5 probably
6 noticeably

Activities 1–7
1 **a** slowly but surely
   b really and truly
   c Yours faithfully
   d Yours sincerely
2 **a** geologically
   b technologically
   c psychologically
   d pathologically
   e physiologically
   f meteorologically
   g biologically
3 Some answers are:
   Adverbs from words ending in -ic:
   comically   strategically
   academically   eccentrically
   graphically   athletically   scenically
   harmonically
   Adverbs from words ending in -ical:
   hypothetically   methodically
   practically   tactically   cynically
   mathematically   sceptically
   politically   fanatically   clinically
   periodically
4 immediately   accidentally
   probably   unnecessarily   basically
   definitely   incidentally   terrifically
5 Undoubtedly   subtly   wittily
   particularly   extremely   successfully
6 **a** truly   faithfully   sincerely
   b carefully   methodically
      successfully
   c frantically   crazily   tragically
   d romantically   desperately
      completely
   e naturally   automatically
      accurately
   f coolly   serenely   gracefully
   g terrifically   fantastically
      incredibly
   h simply   beautifully   unforgettably
7 satisfactorily   particularly   hastily
   apologetically   unspeakably
   haughtily   definitely   loftily
   completely   dreamily   Extremely
   simply   unnecessarily   pathetically
   positively   gloomily   undoubtedly
   obstinately   unbearably   wearily

ANSWERS

Choosing the right ending
(page 70)
Checkpoint A
1. **a** obstacle
   b practical
   c vertical
   d cubicle
   e surgical
   f clerical
   g critical
2. **a** character
   b solicitor
   c calculator

Checkpoint B
1. factory
2. centenary
3. inventory
4. veterinary
5. estuary
6. refectory

Checkpoint C
1. prevention
2. pretension
3. omission
4. apprehension
5. profession
6. persuasion

Checkpoint D
1. melodious
2. advantageous
3. famous
4. religious
5. glorious
6. ferocious
7. grievous
8. hideous
9. previous
10. self-righteous

Checkpoint E
1. **a** eloquent
   b prominent
   c excellent
   d inelegant
   e relevant
2. **a** consequence
   b conference
   c perseverance
   d persistence
   e sentence

Checkpoint F
1. horrible
2. indigestible
3. irresistible
4. uncontrollable
5. probable
6. responsible
7. noticeable
8. comprehensible
9. eligible
10. incredible
11. unforgettable
12. indestructible

Activities 1–4
1. excellent outrageous furious miracle gorgeous spectacle calendar
2. characters imaginary author emperor conqueror voluntary donor sponsor professor doctor politician solicitor governor gardener surveyor beggar monastery cellar burglar vehicle maintenance supervisor miscellaneous library mischievous caterpillar lavatory attendant cemetery laboratory technician veterinary sponsored
3. dictionary's indispensable comprehensible familiar similar peculiar relevance technical competence grammar sentence persistence
4. vehicle identical technical tentacle expense maintenance immense mountainous scenery feasible visible disposable indispensable religious existence sentence ridiculous

Plurals (page 78)
Checkpoint A
1. boxes
2. princesses
3. recipes
4. survivors
5. metaphors
6. pitches
7. witches
8. businesses

Checkpoint B
1 supplies
2 lollies
3 enquiries
4 families

Checkpoint C
1 donkeys
2 volleys
3 trolleys
4 diaries
5 convoys
6 factories
7 pulleys
8 estuaries
9 jockeys
10 centuries
11 libraries
12 universities
13 facilities
14 holidays

Activities 1–6
1 knives recipes jellies pastries boxes glasses tomatoes biros potatoes loaves lollies
2 **a** properties
  b trolleys
  c families
  d journeys countries
  e replies
  f valleys
  g witches prophecies
  h chimneys factories
  i tries penalties
  j heroes heroines
  k apologies
3 Ending -ies: rallies cemeteries allies sundries libraries
  Ending -eys: alleys chimneys valleys
  Others: echoes roofs gigolos potatoes thieves sandwiches take-offs
4 **a** fourteen giraffes
  b forty monkeys
  c eight bush babies
  d eighteen ponies
  e eighty donkeys
  f ninety calves
5 **a** ivies cactuses (or cacti) daisies grasses lilies irises narcissi (or narcissuses) gladioli (or gladioluses) cypresses birches

  b lorries batteries shelves dinghies jerseys armies navies
  c secretaries dictionaries universities facilities enquiries
6 heroes survivors crises catastrophes mosquitoes gases volcanoes

A summary of endings
(page 83)
Activities 1–4
1 **a** mimicking
  b preferring
  c noticing
  d omitting
  e arguing
  f tying
  g flying
  h appealing
  i hoeing
  j appalling
  k surveying
  l panicking
2 Category 1: occurring committed preferred beginning
  Category 2: propelled modelling travelling
  Category 3: swimming shinned
  Category 4: offering benefited budgeted riveting
  Category 5: applying carrying
  Category 6: repeated
  Category 7: delayed
  Category 8: dining staring devising
3 **a** immediately applicants relevant successful marketing experience preferably salary dependent experience accompanied addresses referees
  b successful applicant responsible statutory agencies voluntary sectors programmes strategically committees secretarial advantageous travelling expenses paid
  c voluntary centre handicapped applicant familiar committed physically handicapped preference applicants

technically proficient driving
licence particularly valuable
excellent facilities available
initially offered temporary
permanent

4 a typically extravagant
legendary heroes easily
magically scenically beautiful
characters forgettable

b critically phenomenally
successful physically
handicapped Director fulfilling
compelling performances

c exceptionally vicious
horrifically repellent murderer
outrageous violence

d irresistibly humorous
glamorous fantasies
gorgeously subtly wittily
definitely

Punctuation and spelling
(page 89)

Checkpoint A

1 a the girl's hair
b the girls' hair
c the ship's cargo
d the ships' cargoes
e the English team's efforts
f the children's toys
g three weeks' holiday
h the babies' crying
i a whole month's work
j the mice's tails

2 a there's   we're
b won't   it's
c I'd
d It's
e doesn't it
f you're

Checkpoint B

Dear	first word
Jane	name – proper noun
Simon	name – proper noun
It's	start of new sentence
Wednesday	day of the week – proper noun
August	month – proper noun
Spain	country – proper noun
We	start of new sentence
Marbella	place – proper noun
BA	initial letters of British Airways
Paradise Beach	place – proper noun
There	start of new sentence
English	nationality
Spanish	nationality
Germans	nationality
Dutch	nationality
The	start of new sentence
Umber Solero	product name – proper noun
I'm (twice)	pronoun 'I' always written as a capital letter
Love	word in book title
Shore	word in book title
All	start of new sentence
Do	start of speech
The	start of new sentence
No	start of speech
See	start of new sentence
Mandy	name – proper noun

English, Spanish, Germans, Dutch: adjectives derived from proper nouns

Checkpoint C

1 In front of the French greengrocer's shop there were notices in English advertising Cox's Orange Pippins, William pears and Seville oranges.

2 It's not his or hers but theirs.

3 As he's just out of hospital he cannot go upstairs or downstairs straightaway but tomorrow he may be able to.

Activities 1–4

1 a fifty-odd (about 50)   fifty odd (50 strange)

b big-vehicle owners (people who own big vehicles)   big vehicle-owners (big people who own vehicles)

c all most (everyone was helpful)   almost (nearly helpful)

d re-covered (have another cover put on)   recovered (found)

e Man eating shark (a man is eating the shark)   man-eating shark (a shark that eats men)

2 dog-tired   no one's   doesn't   they're   retrievers   Yorkshire   Irish   their   it's   butchers'   dog-in-the-manger   lets   tomorrow   Let's   its   yours   in front   in between   a lot of   yours   as well   it's   dog's   maybe   cannot   English

3 I'm Joan English Business
Studies Bradchester College My
June Gemini My Friday My
Caribbean Mediterranean
Sometimes I The Independent
The Guardian The I Coronation
Street I Scotsmen Welshmen
I Christmas I Victorian

4 tomorrow don't what's I've
can't although in fact I'm in
spite doesn't work's I've I'm
I've a lot of course what's
I've there's doesn't as well
don't won't

250 key words (page 96)
Activities 1–5
1 among friends paid balance
immediately views bargains
until necessary building across
coming quarter thorough
favourite speech

2 • Exciting development
• Concentrated effect
• Really disappear immediately
• woollens beautifully finished
• Guaranteed fibre-friendly
environmentally
• quarter
• Recommended

3 desperate embarrassed
disastrous appalling loose
tyranny seize opportunity
success guaranteed skilful
technique vicious villains
rhythm accommodation succumb

4 Personnel February chemical
development technician
advertisement Independent
eighteen interested develop
knowledge interest scientific
particularly passed achieving
passed Language Mathematics
Computer especially welcome
opportunity acquire further
referred advertisement
experience laboratory holiday
involved apparatus carrying
chemical preparations monitoring
current planning department
Council chiefly clerical develop

technical field further necessary
Yours faithfully

5 Speech Council receive speak
grateful opportunity address
Council among said there
different opposing views
thorough quarters argument
allowed Forest natural offered
scheme believe exaggerated
relief business paid planning
decisions permission
development believe devastating
effect environment

Further activities (page 103)
Activities 1–19
1 a woollens sandals women's
handkerchiefs men's pyjamas
scissors furniture
b Barbecue here tomorrow
Wednesday weather
permitting
c gratefully received
d Tuesday's Tomorrow
Parliament Neighbours Friends
Families Favourites Defence
Nuclear Deterrent Opportunity
Across Arctic Eskimos View
Environment Caribbean
e potatoes tomatoes vegetable
lettuce sausages barbecue
biscuits desiccated coconut
margarine mayonnaise
cigarettes

2 a unforgettably
b undoubtedly
c disappearance
d unnaturally
e overruled
f unscientifically
g disappointment

3 acknowledge receipt twelfth
February (2 mistakes) dispatched
carriage paid freight supplier
Assuring immediate Yours
faithfully

4 truly subtle irresistible
fragrance internationally
renowned wholly natural
ingredients specially recipe
vacuum laboratories favourite
refrigerator

5 vehicle maintenance carried professional mechanics diesel speciality accelerator pedal anti-freeze transmission alternator exhaust punctured tyre panelling

6 Crossword
Across: 4 excited   6 fulfilled
8 tragedy   11 offered
12 accidentally
Down: 1 separately   2 scene
3 business   5 undoubtedly
6 friend   7 general   9 Arctic
10 lose

7 athletics colonel assistant commissioner police author surveyor college principal doctor medicine field marshal foreign mechanic gardener government inspector laboratory technician librarian councillor lieutenant editor marriage counsellor mathematician meteorologist environment mortgage nuclear physicist personnel police superintendent politician parliament priest professor literature psychiatrist psychologist religious knowledge sergeant shepherd soldier solicitor's secretary speech

8 address experience accommodation responsible liaison secretary personnel secretarial assistant government planning department secretarial college tertiary college technical college interests committee leisure centre involved swimming maintenance facilities.

9 a valuable opportunity acquire prestigious business premises offering excellent accommodation luxury apartments professionals neighbouring leisure facilities
b advertisement particularly spacious thatched character cottage beautiful views
c attractive semi-detached maisonette attached separate dining manageable

10 a unnecessarily
b occasionally
c disadvantageous
d accompaniment
e uncharacteristically
f aggressively
g unnoticeable
h uncontrollable
i regrettably
j cancellations
k irresponsibly
l successfully

11 a Traveller's variety environment equatorial forest plateau capital neighbouring volcanoes approximately metres height tropical valleys estuary atmosphere temperatures Fahrenheit relatively government efficient travelling Islands laboratory recommended visitor truly phenomenal barren scenery
b bored Britain holidaying Caribbean Portuguese sunning Mediterranean island Cyprus travelling Hungary Czech exciting Arctic experience

12 Wordsearch:
Across: definite finite conscious apparatus exhibit separate skilful
Down: disrupt excite preparatory science assign accept infinity conscience

13 cemetery sacrilege vicar weird practices rumoured occurred cemetery neighbouring families happenings seems worshipping primitive idols blasphemy religious communities condemned outrageous exaggerated mischievous residents alcohol attracted travellers hymns psalms said travellers exaggerated prejudice having

14 College Mathematics conscientious committed scholar whose successes arithmetic statistics unparalleled teaching (experience is correct!) English

Literature undoubtedly subtlety critical ability marshal relevant reference as well analyse argument privilege teach Physics truly remarkable concentration particularly efficient skilful appliance scientific techniques using laboratory apparatus complimented (praised) excellence achievements academically athletics field grateful to valuable college disciplinary committee College Principal

15 Crossword

Across: 1 unforgettably   3 occurred
6 chief   8 scene   9 seize
10 absence   12 niece
13 knowledgeably

Down: 1 unnecessary   2 received
4 referring   5 immediately
7 believe   8 sentence   11 sill

16 eight   seized   opportunity premier   league   exciting inspired   disciplined   devastating aggression   opposition condemned   quiet   quarter favourite   welcome   deceived four   defence   slotted   safely Eighteen   minutes   skilful   chief received   carefully   laid-off dispatch   fiercely   past   rhythm further   exciting   bicycle ricocheted   deceive   minutes apparently   oblivious   guilty

appalling   gratefully   snapped clinical   volleys   aggression irresistible   further   scoring marvellous   subtle   relieved visitors   wondered   temporary relief   persistence   denied   further embarrassment   skilfully   desperate opposition   succession   eightieth minute   mightily   Finally   ecstatic fourth   campaign   beginning

17 Spell quiz game

18 Community   controversial contemporary   consensus   among politicians   parties   government's parliamentary   jeopardy   believing views   constituents   developments prejudicial   sovereignty bureaucracy   negotiate   Britain opponents   emphasise concentration   commercial   offered community   viewed   universally beneficial   commitment   defence maintenance   invaluable   targeting significant

19 description   patient   forty   patient admitted   suffering   hypothermia abnormally   temperature pneumonia   laboratory   protein deficiency   patient   stomach diarrhoea   patient   eighty   patient suffering   rheumatism   asthma hypersensitive   physiotherapy patient   eight   patient   catarrh eczema   inoculated   diphtheria hyperactive   psychiatric